The SHOE

The SHOE

Willie Shoemaker's Illustrated Book of Racing

by Willie Shoemaker & Dan Smith

RAND MᶜNALLY & COMPANY   Chicago / New York / San Francisco

PHOTOGRAPHS REPRODUCED COURTESY OF THE FOLLOWING:
Tibor Abahazy; George Andrus; Arlington Park; Joseph W. Burnham; California Thoroughbred Breeders' Association; Caufield-Shook, Inc.; *Chicago Tribune;* Churchill Downs; Jerry Cooke; Del Mar Thoroughbred Club; Frank De Vol; El Monte Union High School; Michael Gill; Golden Gate Fields; Mrs. H. A. Guidera; Marshall Hawkins; Hollywood Turf Club; Allen W. Hopkins; Robert Kingsbury; *Los Angeles Times;* Los Angeles Turf Club; *Louisville Courier-Journal;* Bill Mochon; New York Racing Association; Paul Oxley; *Pasadena Star-News;* William Scherlis; Sheedy & Long; Herb Shoebridge; *Sports Illustrated* photographs © Time, Inc.; Sunland Park; Turf Paradise; United Press International; Vic Stein & Associates; Wide World

Book Design by MARIO PAGLIAI

Copyright © 1976 by WILLIAM SHOEMAKER

All rights reserved

Printed in the UNITED STATES of AMERICA
by RAND McNALLY & COMPANY

First printing, 1976

Library of Congress Cataloging in Publication Data
Shoemaker, Willie.
    The SHOE.

    Includes index.
    1. Shoemaker, Willie.   2. Jockeys—United States—Biography.   I. Smith, Dan, 1936-
joint author.   II. Title.   III. Title: Illustrated Book of Racing.
SF336.S47A37   798'.43'0924 [B]   76-46368
ISBN 0-528-81845-7

Overleaf: Crimson Satan and Shoemaker winning the 1961 Garden State Stakes at Garden State Park. Donut King, with Don Pierce aboard, was second; Obey, with Howard Grant riding, was third.—*Author's Collection*

Preceding overleaf: The horses break out of the gate for the running of the 1962 Belmont Stakes, won by Jaipur (4), with "The Shoe" aboard, in one of the tightest finishes in the history of this event. —*Author's Collection*

Contents

EDDIE ARCARO—"*Regardless of the particular sport, Bill Shoemaker, by his accomplishments, must be considered one of the outstanding athletes in the history of sports. I doubt we'll ever see another race rider having his special combination of talents. He has it all and has done it all. THE SHOE is required reading for all fans of Thoroughbred racing, including this one.*"

JOHN LONGDEN—"*It's difficult to say enough about Bill Shoemaker. Both on and off the racetrack, he's the greatest. He's a great rider and a great gentleman. I said when he broke my record for winners in 1970 at Del Mar that it took a helluva man to set the record and it took a helluva man to break it. And that still holds true today.*"

Right: Damascus and "The Shoe" in the winner's circle following the 1967 Belmont Stakes.—*Author's Collection*

The SHOE

—*Photo by Jerry Cooke*

"I Almost Didn't Make It"

MY FAMILY LIVED near the town of Fabens, Texas, which is about 30 miles from El Paso, and I was born at home on August 19, 1931. The story of what happened right after I was born is one my mother told me when I was a kid and my grandmother also told me a couple of times after that.

My Dad was average-sized—about 5-foot-11—and Mom was 5-foot-3½. I arrived a month early and weighed only 2½ pounds at birth. The doctor who delivered me put me on the bed and told my mother I wouldn't live out the night. My grandmother didn't want to accept that, so she took me and put me in a shoe box. She opened the oven, turned on the heat, and put me in there with the door open. It was kind of a homemade incubator, and the next morning I was still alive. I was christened Billy Lee Shoemaker. My brother Lonnie was born about a year later.

We moved around a lot when I was a kid, but I didn't mind it that much. It was the middle of the Depression, and there wasn't much work. My father was trying to find some place to make some money to feed his family. He worked in the cotton mill in Fabens and did odd jobs in different parts of Texas, and when things didn't work out he either got fired or he quit. Then, when I was seven, I went to live with my grandparents for a couple of years on a cattle and sheep ranch near Winters, which isn't far from Abilene [Texas]. My grandfather was the manager of the ranch. He had a big horse, and I used to ride to the end of the road where the mailbox was to get the mail and bring it back. And that was my big thing for the day.

I was close to my grandparents and I enjoyed that ranch, I really enjoyed it. But once I almost drowned there. They had these big tanks where the cattle came to drink, and I was walking along and fell right into one of them. I didn't know how to swim, and I didn't know what to do to get out. I just remember floating. One of my aunts saw me coming up for the third time and got me out. For the second time in my life, I almost didn't make it. She squeezed all the water out of my lungs, and I survived again. I was gone. Really, I wouldn't have made it. She caught me just in time.

I went to a little country school near Winters. Winters was the biggest town in the area, but it was quite a ways from where we lived. I didn't really like school that much. I'd rather have been back at the ranch riding that horse. On many days, I didn't even go to school. I'd just take off and go up in the hills and do something. Times were kind of tough when I was a kid, but I think I really learned to appreciate life.

While I was living with my grandparents, my mother and father got a divorce. My Dad remarried and moved to California and then sent for Lonnie and me. So then we came to California to live with him and my stepmother. I was about ten years old—it was right after

the start of the war. My father had gone there to work in the factories, and when the war came along you could get jobs easy and the pay was good. When I got to California, I had to go to school because they were stricter and the laws were different. I went to Baldwin Park grade school and after that to El Monte Union High School.

I wasn't into sports too much in Texas. We played a little soccer, but it wasn't really soccer, we just kind of kicked the ball around. When I was a little older, I was more competitive in sports, and in high school I got into wrestling and boxing. First though, I went out for football, only I was too little. I couldn't find shoes small enough to fit, and the shoulder pads were all too big. I didn't make the team because the coach was weeding the players out. So I tried basketball, but the coach said I was too short—"Out!" I guess I weighed about 80 pounds.

But I was determined to compete in some sport in school, and when I heard about the wrestling and boxing teams, I thought I'd go out for them. The lightest there was the 95- to 105-pound class, and that's what I tried for. And I was good. I beat all those guys who weighed 95 pounds, so I wound up as the team leader of my division at school. We traveled to

Left: Flexing his muscles impressively, Shoemaker, fifth from left in bottom row, was an 80-pound mighty mite on the wrestling team at El Monte Union High School in 1947. A champion in Golden Gloves boxing, he also was unbeaten as a high school wrestler.—*From the school yearbook, "Trail's End"*

Right: Already the dedicated athlete while still a teenager attending high school, Billy Shoemaker, as he was known then, displays his muscular development.—*Author's Collection*

other schools in the San Gabriel Valley for meets, and that year—1945—the team was unde-feated. In fact, I never lost a match, boxing or wrestling, right through the time I quit school in the 11th grade. I must have had ten matches a year, at least, and I was unbeaten in the conference and in practice too. The closest I came to losing was in a wrestling match once when I was tied. It was a dead heat. It's funny, but I had confidence and knew I could do it. People would look at me and probably say, "That poor little guy, no way he can compete with these guys." The only thing I could do was get in and show them.

I didn't do that much training before I started competing in high school. I did work with weights a little bit because I had a friend, one of those guys with the big muscles, who used to work out. He said, "Come on, I'll show you how." I said, "All right, let me try it." I did it for a while, but it got boring. When I got into wrestling and boxing, I trained pretty hard, because I liked it. As a wrestler, I was agile and difficult to hold onto. I was fast, and I'd whip around and get on those guys with a half nelson and pin them. There are new methods now and new techniques. The half nelson was my favorite hold. That hold was it. If I ever got that on them, forget it—it was all over. As a boxer, I wasn't big enough to hit hard, although I'll never for-

Left: As a sophomore in 1947 at El Monte Union High School, Shoemaker, at left in bottom row, joined with his Golden Gloves teammates to pose for a picture for the school yearbook, "Trail's End."

get this big skinny kid I fought in the Golden Gloves—the Los Angeles division—when the tournament was held at the El Monte Legion Stadium. I must have hit him 20 times and he was staggering around, but I never could put him away. I only weighed about 85 pounds, and that skinny kid was about a foot taller. He whacked me around pretty good until I finally worked inside his long reach and got to him, and I won the fight.

I had a good relationship with the guys in school because of what I accomplished in sports. I was champion of the school in my division in both boxing and wrestling, and I was popular because of it. Not with the girls, though. I don't know, the girls didn't like me for some reason—too little or something, I guess.

There was a girl named Joyce in one of my classes when I was a freshman who was dating Wallace (Bud) Bailey, a jockey. She told me I should be a jockey, and I said, "What's that?" I didn't know anything about it, but after she explained it to me I said I'd like to try it. She said she'd introduce me to her boyfriend and make him help get me started. And she did. He probably didn't want to, but she conned him into it. He took me out to the Suzy Q Ranch, which was a Thoroughbred farm in Puente, and got me a job. I worked at the ranch in the morning and at night after school for quite a while. My father didn't know it, but in my junior year I transferred from El Monte to La Puente High School. Then I got tired of going to school, and finally I stopped going altogether. Instead, I'd get up at five in the morning and go to the ranch, work there all day, and come home at night just like I'd been to school. My Dad didn't know what I'd been doing until almost the end of the school year, when I told him I was leaving home to go live at the ranch permanently. He was a little mad at first, but then he decided, "What the hell, I can't do anything about it now. It's too late. He wants to do this, so I'll let him." I was making $75 a month, plus room and board, at the ranch—big money for a kid of 16.

A 16-year-old exercise boy with dreams of being a professional race rider, Shoemaker was a member of the Turf Boys Club in 1948 at Hollywood Park, playing pool and living with other youngsters who shared his ambitions.—*Author's Collection*

"The Kid Gets with It"

AS SOON AS I began working at the Suzy Q Ranch, I knew I'd found my niche in life. It was great being around horses all the time, and I loved it, all of it. Like on a regular ranch, we did everything. I started in by cleaning out stalls the first thing, which you do, and I enjoyed that even, actually got a big kick out of it. I'd really get in there and muck out all the stalls on one side of a barn, and the guy'd say, "The kid really gets with it. He got this job done sooner than I could have." We had the racetrack to take care of too. We harrowed it and watered it and hauled all the hay in from the fields in wagons to feed the horses. Then I began working with the horses more, cooling them out after they'd been to the track getting up on them and riding them, and finally breaking yearlings.

When I started breaking yearlings, I couldn't wait to get thrown the first time. It was a badge of merit or courage to be thrown off. It didn't happen for a couple of days, and I was getting a little disappointed that a horse hadn't bucked me off. But then one did, and after that I got busted 40 times a day, and every time a horse threw me off I thought it was fun. I got a kick out of it.

Right from the word go, I just knew I wanted to be a rider. I knew I had to work hard to impress on people that I was serious about what I wanted to be. I figured if I worked hard and showed an interest, they would show an interest in me. And I loved it, and that made it a lot easier.

They had an old jock working there at the ranch—he'd probably been ruled off every track in the country—one of those old riders who'd been broken up and walked funny. He started out by showing me how to cross the reins and get down on a horse. I didn't even know how to get down on a horse; all the time I was just standing up in the irons and galloping. The first horse I broke from the gate was part of a team working out of the gate. We went about 30 yards, and he bolted and went through the outside fence. When I came up out of the ditch, I had the bridle in my hand and I was a little disgusted. I said, "Is this the way this thing is supposed to work?"

I really enjoyed the ranch. It was a great place to live, and they fed you three meals a day. I probably was heavier there than I've ever been. I got up to about 102 pounds eating all the pies and everything. It was great food. Tom Simmons, who was president of Hollywood Park, owned the ranch, but I didn't really get to know him too well. He didn't come around too often. Once in a while he would walk through there, and everybody would stand at attention.

Getting my foundation at that ranch probably was the best thing that ever happened to me. It was better than anything I could think of to advise a young guy to do if he wants to become a rider. It's the best way to learn all about horses, what to do with them in the beginning, and to get a real good feel about them. That's not just like coming to the track and getting on a horse and then a year later you're riding races. You really don't know what the hell the horse is all about. I think Latin riders who come to the United States get the foundation because they go through a period in which they have to do all those things I did when I was young. Here, you have riders who come from the cities and hit the racetracks, and some of them start right in by walking hots, galloping horses, and riding. They don't know anything more basic than that. In any game you get into, if you really want to be successful you have to dedicate yourself. No question about it. And I did dedicate myself. I didn't do anything but try to learn what I was supposed to do. And I worked. Whatever had to be done, I'd work 24 hours a day to do it if I had to. I didn't have any doubts about myself. Of course, I didn't know I was going to be as successful as I was or win as many races as I did. But I knew that I was going to be a rider, and if work and dedication would help make me a good rider, then I would be a good rider.

I worked on the ranch for a couple of years, and then one day Bill Roland, a buddy of mine who also worked on the ranch, said, "Let's go to the races." This was in 1948, and I hadn't turned 17 yet. We went to San Francisco and got into a hotel, and the next morning we headed for Bay Meadows and walked around to see if we could get a job. Hurst Philpot, who was training the horses owned by Charles S. Howard, asked me, "Have you ever galloped a horse?" "Yah, lots of them," I told him. He said, "All right, I'll try you." He put me on a filly, took me out, and told me to gallop her once around then pull her up and bring her back. I galloped her around, and she started running off with me. I couldn't stop her. We went by

Right: The Turf Boys Club was Shoemaker's home-away-from-home during the summer of 1948 at Hollywood Park, where he was an exercise boy for trainer Hurst Philpot.—*Author's Collection*

him, and he hollered at me, "Pull her up!" Whew, I couldn't. We went around again. He yelled at me, "Hey, I thought I told you to pull that horse up." And I'm saying to myself, "What do you think I'm trying to do, you dumb son of a bitch." Finally, I got her pulled up and I'm really tired. And then I found out he did it on purpose. He had this mare and he knew she'd run off, and he wanted to do it just for fun. I wound up being one of the best exercise boys he had.

Johnny Adams, who was a top, well-established jock and rode for Hurst Philpot, used to come out in the morning to work horses for Hurst. I learned a lot from John just by watching him ride—how he used his hands and could rate a horse. It was lucky for me he was around at the time because he taught me a lot.

Philpot had two kids working for him named Buddy Heacock and Jimmy Hood, and he was going to make riders out of them. Even though I galloped many of the good horses Hurst trained, he thought I was too little to make a rider. So I said to myself, "I don't think I have much future with this guy." I decided to quit him after the Hollywood Park meeting, and I went to Del Mar by myself. I walked around and got a job with another trainer, George Reeves, who took an apprentice contract on me. He liked me because I worked hard and I got along well with his horses. I galloped a couple of them that ran off with other guys and even got along with these tough horses of his. I think Reeves recognized something in me that Hurst Philpot didn't. Besides, Hurst was busy running a big stable and trying to make riders out of two other young guys. George didn't have too many horses, only ten or 12.

The next winter, early in 1949, at Santa Anita, I was walking a horse on the tow ring one morning when Harry Silbert came to George's barn to hustle a mount for his rider, and George said to Harry, "You see that kid walking that horse? You'd better be his agent. He's going to be a good one someday." Harry said, "Yah, yah, I know." But then he said, "Okay. When you start him riding, call me and let me know, and I'll take his book." Harry knew he was going to lose his rider, Bill Passmore, who was going to leave town or go back East, and Harry wanted to stay home.

They used to have running match races when I first came to the track, and I could run like hell. Bob Cass, who's a bloodstock agent and owns horses, spotted that early and won a lot of bets on me. He told everyone, "That little bastard can really run," but nobody believed him. All the races were 50 or 60 yards. He gave me a watch once for winning a race that he'd bet a couple of hundred on.

A short while later, when we were at Golden Gate Fields, George called Harry and told him he was going to start me out riding. Harry said he'd come up, but then his wife got sick and had to have an operation so he couldn't come just then. George told him, "I'll let this other agent have his book until you can get here," which turned out to be the next week or so. I rode my first race on March 19, 1949, at Golden Gate, going three-quarters of a mile on a filly named Waxahachie, and we finished fifth. Waxahachie, trained by George, was a good-natured old mare that I knew pretty well because I galloped her every morning. I didn't think I was nervous, but I guess I must have been. I was supposed to wear two pairs of goggles because the track was muddy, but I forgot and wore only one. Waxahachie didn't have much speed so we were outrun during the first part of the race, and with the mud flying back in my face, I couldn't see a damned thing. I pulled down my goggles, which were all muddy, and then I realized I'd forgotten the second pair. Fortunately, that old mare was smart and experienced, and she got me around there okay.

Another thing I remember about that first race is that John Longden and Gordon Glisson got into an argument after it was over. Longden had shut me off coming out of the gate. He was on the outside and came over and got me in the first race I ever rode. And because it was my first race, I didn't even realize he had done it. But Glisson jumped all over Longden. "What the hell you shutting that kid off for? The first race he rides, and you had to stop him coming out of the gate." Longden said, "I didn't mean to," and they went on arguing over it. I'm saying to myself, "Shhh, boys, don't fight, it didn't bother me." And they almost did get into a fight over Longden shutting me off.

The second horse I rode was a 90–1 shot named Soonuseeme, and we came in fourth. My third race was on Shafter V. on April 20, and she became my first winner. Shafter V. had won the week before with an older rider named R. J. Martin when she was 4–5. She was back

Right: Riding in only his third race, apprentice Shoemaker gets his first winner, on Shafter V., at Golden Gate Fields, April 20, 1949. At left in the winner's circle after the historic moment is trainer George Reeves.—*Photos courtesy of Mrs. H. A. Guidera*

in with the same horses and the same kind of race, and she should have been 4–5 again but instead was 9–1 with me on her. All the guys at the barn got well because they bet on her. Before the race, the stewards called George in and wanted to know why he was putting a green kid on a 4–5 shot, because I'd ridden in only two races and the "public will be betting on him and you shouldn't be doing this." George said, "I have confidence in him and I think he can ride her and I think she'll win." He talked them into leaving me on her, and it worked. I was pretty excited about winning my first race. I remember that when I got off Shafter V. in the winner's circle, my knees buckled and gave out on me. I was still a little shaky in the legs walking back to the jocks' room.

During about the second week I rode, I won seven races and Harry had me and we got going. And that was it, we never stopped. When I first came around though, everybody said, "This kid never moves on a horse, what the hell is he doing?" I didn't know I wasn't moving. I better take a look, I thought, because I felt I was doing fine until somebody mentioned me never moving on a horse. But when I took a look I knew I was okay, because I could see that I wasn't whipping and slashing and jumping around like the other riders. "I don't know how to ride like that, so I'll just have to do the best I can with what I have," I told myself. I started winning races and horses ran for me. Sort of difficult to criticize success, but I had my critics. They talked to George most of the time—no one ever really said anything to me personally. In a kind of roundabout way to George, they'd say, "That kid doesn't know how to ride, why don't you put somebody else on that horse?" And I got beat on a lot of horses that maybe I shouldn't have. George would tell them, "No, that's my rider, and I'm going to stick with him." And he did. He sure was a good man and he helped me so much in my career. I won 219 races as an apprentice in 1949, even though I didn't get started until April, and I was second in the nation that year to Gordon Glisson.

Left top: Shoemaker and an early rival for apprentice honors, Glen Lasswell, good-naturedly square off at Del Mar during the 1949 summer season.—*Los Angeles Times*

Left bottom: Gordon Glisson, America's leading rider in number of winners in 1949, and Willie Shoemaker, who finished second to Glisson although still an apprentice, discuss their trade in the Hollywood Park jockeys' room in 1950.—*Vic Stein & Associates*

Riding at Agua Caliente on the last day of 1950, Shoemaker recorded his 388th win of the year aboard Bust Out, trained by Bobby Warren, right, to tie Joe Culmone as champion jockey for total number of victories.—*Wide World*

"Silent Shoe"

I GOT THE TAG "Silent Shoe" in the beginning, but I didn't pay much attention to it. I could talk if I wanted to, but I just figured I was better off listening because I didn't know that much and the guy who listens is the guy who learns, not the guy talking. I guess I was pretty mature in my attitudes for my age. Even when I was in high school I was fairly mature, more so than the average 16-year-old. It'd be nice if all kids could know what they wanted to do in life at that age. I was fortunate I did know.

When I was a bug boy—an apprentice, that is—Harry Silbert asked me to go to Agua Caliente and ride on Sundays for the experience. So I rode seven days a week for a long time. I'd ride nine races each weekday and then 12 more on Sundays at Caliente. I enjoyed it, but it was for experience too. The more you ride the better you get. Harry felt I needed that extra riding to polish me out and make me a professional. Some of the things I did on a horse he didn't like. And he was right. He knew what he was looking at and talking about. I was backward in certain areas, and I needed a lot more experience.

There were three apprentices at Santa Anita early in 1950: Bill Boland, who came out from the East, Glen Lasswell, and me. Lasswell looked the best. He looked better on a horse than I did, and he probably was better at the time. I said to myself, "He's a better rider than I am, but I'm going to keep trying and maybe I'll improve and get there." And it didn't take me too long to get it together. At first, for one thing, I didn't really know how to push on a horse. I just kind of sat there and chirped to the horse. Finally, it started coming, and the more I rode the more the feeling came. Knowing what to do and how to do it and when to do it

Above: Nineteen-year-old Willie Shoemaker and John Longden shake hands after they tied for the Del Mar riding championship with 60 winners each in 1950.—*Del Mar*

Right: Child actress Margaret O'Brien was in the winner's circle at Del Mar to welcome Imperium and jockey Willie Shoemaker after their win in the Bing Crosby Handicap in 1950.—*Del Mar*

with the horse—it all began to fall into place. From the start though, I had a good idea of where I was on the racetrack. I had no problems there.

I lost the five-pound apprentice allowance in April of 1950, but for most of the year I was the leading rider for winners. Joe Culmone was another jock who was having a great year. I went to Bowie, Maryland, one day to ride against Culmone in a series of races. It was cold—it must have been early in the spring because I remember the snow on the ground. I'd never ridden in the snow in my whole life, and it was a little different. The first race I rode, I won, in front all the way, and Culmone said it was the first horse that had been in front all the way and won during the whole meeting. The track was deep and cuppy. I said to myself, "That makes me feel good. I have a chance now." The rest of the day I didn't win any, and I think he won about six. We had a match race in between, and he won that one too, by about a hundred yards. He was the victor there, but I went home with a lot of friends, people in the press and others who liked the way I conducted myself. Even though Bowie was a disaster as far as riding was concerned, it was good in many other ways.

Early in the year, Harry and I hadn't given much thought to me being leading rider. We were trying to win as many races as we could to get going and get established. But sometime during the year, we looked up and I was in front, leading rider with the most win-

Right: Riding at Tanforan in 1950, Shoemaker took time out to pose for a picture on the roof of the jockeys' room.—*Author's Collection*

Below: A keen student of his profession from the beginning of his career, "The Shoe" watches a race from atop the jockeys' room at Tanforan in 1950 along with three fellow riders: Grant Zufelt, left; Bill Pearson, right; and Arthur Martinez, rear.—*Author's Collection*

ners. "What the hell, if we're in front we might as well try to win the whole thing." Then, near the end of the year, Culmone caught up to me. He and I were tied going into the final day of 1950, and I went to Caliente and Culmone went to Cuba to ride. He was on several favorites in Cuba. They had 12 races at Caliente, and I think I was on 12 favorites there. We each won three races and wound up tied with 388 winners. That equaled a record set by Walter Miller back in 1906.

After the year I'd just had, people saw I could ride and they wanted me to ride their horses. About this time I hooked on with Red McDaniel, who was the leading trainer in America for winners. That was a stroke of luck. I began riding for him, and we won many races together. McDaniel was the first trainer in the western part of the country who could really read a condition book. I saw it, and just about everyone else had the same opinion. He could claim a horse and figure the horse was going to win a certain race three or four weeks later and he'd enter him in a couple of races in between, and this would work out for Red. If the horse went bad or Red felt the horse wasn't doing well, he'd drop him down in class. He'd claim the horse for $10,000, and he'd run him for $5,000. He trained for owners who let him do that. McDaniel never said much in the paddock before a race. "Just ride him, he'll win, don't worry about it," is about all he'd say to you. He had that kind of confidence in himself or in his horse. The race didn't always turn out the way he thought it would, but most of the time it did.

Aboard Great Circle, Shoemaker wins his first
$100,000 stakes race, the 1951 Santa Anita Maturity.
—*Vic Stein & Associates*

Later on McDaniel had some good horses, like Poona II. I remember he ran Poona in the San Fernando Stakes in 1955 and I was on him, and he ran a big race, won in track-record time. The next time he ran, right before the Santa Anita Handicap, he got beat. Well, Evan Shipman, who was a well-known turf writer from New York, said about Red in an article he did, "This guy knows something about claiming horses, but he doesn't know anything about how to train a good horse." McDaniel really blew his top. Then Poona came back and we won the Santa Anita Handicap, and Red said, "Where is this guy? I want to talk to him, this writer from New York."

From the beginning, when I talked to the press, I tried to give them a good honest answer and to tell them whatever they wanted to know. If they asked me to describe a race, or maybe a part of it, I'd stick with the facts and not say anything derogatory about anyone. Harry used to advise me sometimes. He'd say, "Now this guy is going to interview you. If he asks you this, don't be afraid to say this or that." Nine times out of ten I'd forget what he told me, or I didn't want to say it that way, anyway. I'd say it the way I wanted.

I stayed at George Reeves' barn, in the tack room, most of the time when I first started out. Then I went to live with Harry and his family in their house in La Jolla during the Del Mar meeting. But I didn't get to do much while I was there, because Harry made sure I was in the house. Once in a while, I'd sneak out. I got out one night and went to the beach

with a bunch of kids, and I stepped on a stingray in the water and it stung me on the foot. That poison got to me in a hurry, and I threw up and felt weak and I thought I was going to die. It felt like someone was sawing on my leg all night. It really hurt. The next morning my foot was blown up, and I couldn't put my foot in a boot. I was on some live horses that day, and I said to Harry, "I don't think I'm going to be able to ride." He said, "Oh yah, you'll ride. Don't worry about that. I'll find a boot for you to wear." And he did. He made Dunice DuBois, my valet, bring a boot out, and he slit it open and got it on my foot. I won four races that day.

Right: Shoemaker awaits the call "Riders Up" in the walking ring at Santa Anita.—*Michael Gill*

Below: Checking over the condition book at Hollywood Park during the 1951 racing season are agent Harry Silbert, Shoemaker, and trainer Harry Daniels. —*Vic Stein & Associates*

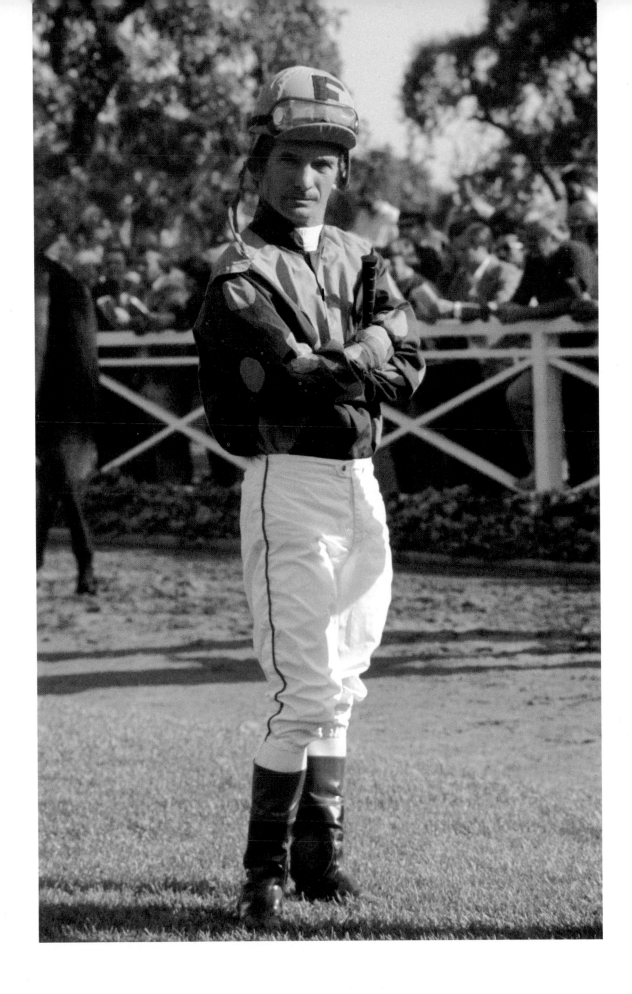

Harry was instrumental in keeping me doing what I was supposed to do, not letting me be distracted by other things, and he did a helluva job. Which is the right way to go. I never resented it, because I knew Harry was right. Sure I liked to go out once in a while, but even though I did sneak out now and then, I knew he was right about me getting my rest and staying in training. I didn't think about luxuries, I thought about my profession and winning. The only luxury I had in those early days was an automobile. One day when I came out of the jocks' room after the last race and walked to the parking lot with Harry, all of a sudden he stopped and said, "There it is." "What?" I asked. "It's your new car," he said. He'd bought me a Buick Riviera. It was a big, shiny car to me. I really got a kick out of that. First car I owned was a Model A Ford I bought with the money I earned at the Suzy Q Ranch. I paid $150 for it. I didn't even have a driver's license, but I drove it anyway. From the start, the bright-lights part of being in racing never tempted me that much. It just didn't move me.

In 1951, I was riding Great Circle for trainer Warren Stute in this tune-up for the Santa Anita Maturity, and going down the backstretch I noticed this jock was in trouble. Either his stirrup broke or his saddle slipped, and he looked like he was going to fall off. I rode up to help him get back into the middle of his horse, and then I went on and finished second. I came back and said, "Sorry, Warren, but this guy looked like he was in trouble and I had to help him. It probably cost me the race." He said, "Well, those things happen." Stute thought Ralph Neves was going to ride Great Circle in the Maturity anyway. But Ralph couldn't make up his mind and didn't give him the right answer or didn't tell him in time, and Stute said, "I'll put this kid back on him." So I rode Great Circle in the Maturity and won, and that was my first win in a hundred-grander. Turning into the stretch in the Maturity, I had moved up from fourth on the backside to third and then second, and when I got to the front, I realized that I had a chance to win. And naturally I was excited because I had never won a race of that caliber.

I went to New York for the first time in 1951. I rode at Santa Anita, went to New York, came back to California for the Hollywood Park season, then back to New York again, and ended the year riding on the West Coast. Eddie Arcaro was one of the reasons I got started so fast in New York. Eddie was acknowledged as the top rider in the country, and his comments about my ability and what he told racing people opened a lot of doors for me. In those days, if you didn't establish yourself at the Big Apple, people didn't consider you a top rider. And that's what I did, and I was leading rider in New York at most of those meetings. I remember Eddie telling me about how Jack Westrope went back to New York from the West Coast and they all were out on the town one night and talking about riders, and Westrope

Left: Swaps and Shoemaker were an almost invincible combination in 1956, when the brilliant chestnut colt was acclaimed Horse of the Year.—*Joseph W. Burnham*

Above: Trainer R. H. (Red) McDaniel, America's leading conditioner in number of winners from 1950 through 1954 and a strong influence on Shoemaker's early career, discusses strategy with the rider in the paddock.—*Author's Collection*

Right: Shoemaker sends handicap ace Moonrush through his paces in a morning workout at Hollywood Park in 1951.—*Vic Stein & Associates*

said, "I'll tell you one thing, there's a little rider in California you never heard of—his name is Shoemaker and he can really ride. You're going to hear a lot about him. He's an apprentice and we're giving him five pounds, and it should be the other way around." And they all said, "Yah, yah, yah." That's the first time Eddie had heard anything about me. "Shoemaker, what does he do? Make shoes?" So Westrope was the first guy who told them in New York about a little rider in California who could really horseback.

I rode at the old Aqueduct track, and I'll never forget my first day there. It was a Saturday, and I was on Thelma Berger in a $50,000 race, the Beldame, for older fillies and mares. Eric Guerin was on the other half of the entry, which supposedly was the better half. But I'd won two other races earlier in the afternoon, and I won the stakes that day when Thelma Berger beat Bed O' Roses. So the first day I rode in New York I won three races, including the stakes. And a $50,000 race back then was a big, big race. That started me right off with a bang.

Above: "The Shoe" wipes his brow after riding a race at Del Mar in the early fifties.—*Del Mar*

Right: Shoemaker and his first wife, Ginny, paid a visit to Your Hostess in her stall at Hollywood Park in 1951.—*Vic Stein & Associates*

When I got to Belmont Park, I couldn't believe how big it was. That's a mile-and-one-half track, and I was used to the mile tracks in California. I was in awe of how big it was. Funny thing about it is you had to be a lot fitter to ride on those sandy tracks than you did in California, because horses labored more and it took more out of you to hold them together and stay with them. You didn't have a pony for each horse. This meant you galloped your horse to the gate by yourself, and the gate was a long ways away. I couldn't ride today if I had to do that—riding six or seven horses and galloping them all the way to the gate, fighting them, and getting them into the gate, and all of it. Riders are fit now, but they had to be a lot fitter then because many of those horses were lunging, diving, and trying to run off, and you had no one to help you. You had to do it yourself. There was one pony boy, and he'd have a hold of a horse, and the rest of them were on their own—that was it. But it made me a better horseman. Riders in general had to be better horsemen than they are today, in the

"Silent Shoe"   39

Right: Shoemaker cuts the cake at a birthday celebration in the Del Mar jockeys' room in the early fifties.—*Del Mar*

Below: John Longden, Shoemaker, and Gordon Glisson picked up baseball gloves to appear with comedian Joe Frisco, second from left, and race caller Joe Hernandez for a baseball game at Del Mar in the early fifties.—*Del Mar*

sense of getting along with the horse. Most jocks today don't know anything about galloping a horse. Take the ponies away from most of these riders and you'd have 40 run-offs every afternoon. This was my first full year without the apprentice allowance, and I ended up leading rider in purses.

In 1953, I rode about 1,600 races and won 485, setting a record for most winners in a year. Compared to today, it's probably not that many. Actually, I quit a couple of weeks before the end of the year. I could have won 500 races. I'm sorry now I didn't go ahead and do it. In two weeks I could have won 15 races easy because I was winning three and four every day. I was a little tired though, and Harry said, "Let's take a couple of weeks off and get ready for Santa Anita. Give you a little rest and freshen up." I had another big year in '54. Out of 1,251 mounts I came in first on 380, and that's more than 30 percent winners, which was the highest percentage for an American rider in the 20th century, I was told.

Above: John Longden's 4,000th winner, in 1952 at Hollywood Park, was a cause for celebration, and joining in was Willie Shoemaker. Almost obscured in the background is Tom Simmons, president of Hollywood Park and owner of the Suzy Q Ranch, where Shoemaker got his start.—*Vic Stein & Associates*

Left top: One of Shoemaker's stakes mounts in the early fifties was Arroz, conditioned by T. W. (Wally) Dunn.—*Vic Stein & Associates*

Left bottom: Under a hand ride by Willie Shoemaker, Arroz wins the 1952 La Jolla Handicap at Del Mar. —*Del Mar*

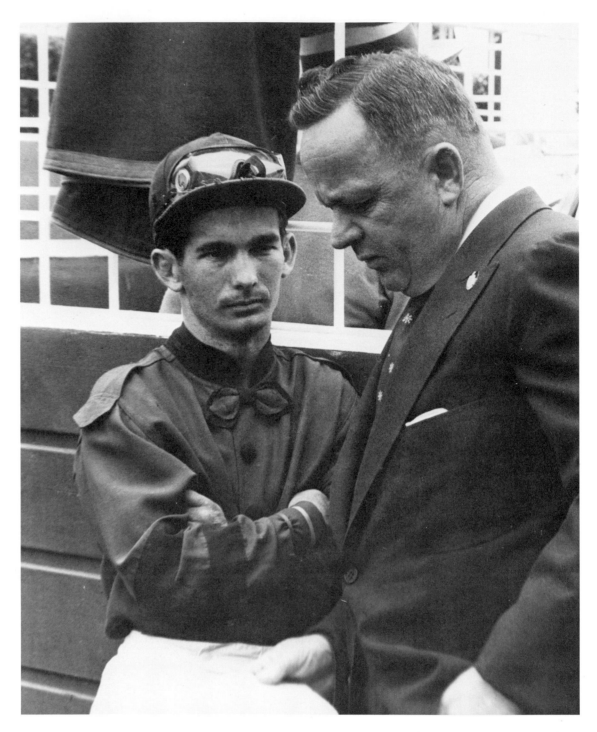

Above: Wearing the silks of Calumet Farm, Shoe-maker listens attentively to trainer Jimmy Jones's instructions in the paddock prior to a stakes event in 1953 at Hollywood Park.—*Vic Stein & Associates*

Right: Willie breaks the Reggie Cornell-trained Damp Abbey from the gate in a workout at Hollywood Park in 1954.—*Vic Stein & Associates*

As a two-year-old, California-bred Swaps, with John Burton up, gave little indication of his tremendous potential, winning two of five starts, including a minor stakes race at Hollywood Park.—*Vic Stein & Associates*

"You're Going to Beat Nashua"

I MENTIONED BEFORE about what a stroke of luck it was hooking up with Red McDaniel. Well, I got lucky again when I became associated with Rex Ellsworth, who was a breeder and owner, and whose stable was on the way up in California in the fifties. The way I started riding for Ellsworth was that he took a train trip from New York up to Boston to watch a race and Eddie Arcaro happened to be on that same train. They were talking, and Rex was telling Eddie, "I've got a barnful of good horses, and I got John Burton and Britt Layton riding them." Eddie said, "Well, that's where you're making a big mistake. If you don't get a guy like Shoemaker riding your horses, you're going to get beat a lot of times when you shouldn't." I guess he was convincing, because Rex contacted Harry, and away we went.

And, of course, riding for Rex Ellsworth and his trainer, Mish Tenney, led me to getting the mount on Swaps. I rode Swaps for the first time in an allowance race at Santa Anita just after the 1954 season started. He won, but I wasn't really too impressed. It was in the San Vicente Stakes early in 1955, when he beat a Calumet Farm horse named Trentonian, that he showed me his potential. I couldn't ride Swaps in the Santa Anita Derby because I'd already obligated myself to ride Blue Ruler, the horse I'd won the Del Mar Futurity on the previous summer. But I was clear after that. Rex and Mish said, "Okay, we'll get somebody else to ride Swaps in the Santa Anita Derby, and then if we go to Kentucky you'll ride him there." Longden rode Swaps in the Santa Anita Derby and won. John thought he was going to ride him back in Kentucky, but Tenney and Ellsworth told him, "No, you can't because we told Shoemaker that if we go to the Kentucky Derby, he's going to ride Swaps."

The Swaps team—owner-breeder Rex Ellsworth, jockey Willie Shoemaker, and trainer M. A. (Mish) Tenney.—*California Thoroughbred Breeders' Association*

Going into the '55 Derby, I didn't know whether Swaps could beat Arcaro's colt, Nashua, who was the big horse from New York. We'd been in California and not running against the same caliber of horse. Still, I figured Swaps probably was the best shot I'd had up to then in the Kentucky Derby. I'd ridden in the Derby for three straight years and hadn't really gotten close. In '52, I rode Count Flame, who was part of an entry with Master Fiddle, and I was fifth to Hill Gail and Arcaro. The next year, I was on a 40–1 shot, Invigorator, and he ran well but we were third, beaten about five lengths. That's the Derby where Dark Star upset Native Dancer. In 1954, I was on Correlation, the favorite, but it was Determine's Derby, and we couldn't get any closer than sixth.

The week before the '55 Derby, I rode Swaps in the Stepping Stone going seven furlongs, and he won easily. After the finish, I worked him on out a mile in 1:36⅖, which in those days nobody had ever done. In fact, Roscoe Goose, who was kind of a legend around Louisville and had won the Derby in 1913 on Donerail, a 90–1 shot, came to me and said, "No horse has ever run in this race and worked out that fast in the history of the Derby. You're on the winner." I said, "Really? That sounds good." He really believed it. He said, "You're going to beat Nashua, and it won't even be a contest." At the time, I didn't see how anyone could say that, knowing Nashua was the big horse from the East and had won all those races. But Roscoe Goose was right. Swaps did whip Nashua.

Top: Swaps and Willie Shoemaker pull away in the final sixteenth of a mile to upset favored Nashua and Eddie Arcaro in the 1955 Kentucky Derby.—*Caufield & Shook, Inc.*

Bottom: Willie Shoemaker doffs his cap in the winner's circle at Churchill Downs after capturing the 1955 Kentucky Derby astride California speedster Swaps.—*Caufield & Shook, Inc.*

Before the Derby, in the paddock, Mish Tenney said to me, "Look, the reason you're riding Swaps is because you're a good rider. We don't know how the race is going to be run, so I'd like for you to be laying second or third if you can. But if it doesn't happen, you have to use your own judgment. And that's why you're riding this horse. You're supposed to be a good rider and use your judgment." Which was kind of smart.

In the race, coming by the stands the first time, I've got a hold on Swaps, but everybody else is taking a hold too. So I just kind of let him ease to the lead, and he relaxed. Down the backside, about the half-mile pole, I said to myself, "Well, if they just let me go a little further like this, they'll never catch me." And that's what happened. Nashua moved up to within about a neck of me turning for home, when Swaps spotted the gate parked to the outside on the track and kind of propped. He stuck his toes in the ground, and that made Nashua get closer than he would have. As soon as I got Swaps straightened away, I clucked to him and hit him, and he just shot away from Nashua by about a length and was pulling away at the finish. Going in, Arcaro probably took Swaps a little lightly. He probably sat back there watching Summer Tan because he thought Summer Tan was the horse to beat.

Above left: Beaten on Nashua, Arcaro congratulates Shoemaker in the Churchill Downs jockeys' room after Swaps won the 1955 Kentucky Derby.—*Author's Collection*

Above right: Willie cools off in the shower after piloting Swaps to an upset triumph over Nashua in the 1955 Kentucky Derby.—*Author's Collection*

Facing page: Candy Spots gave Shoemaker his first success in the Preakness Stakes, middle jewel of racing's Triple Crown, in 1963.—*Marshall Hawkins*

After the Derby, Swaps was shipped back to California to run at Hollywood Park, and Nashua went on to win the Preakness and then the Belmont Stakes. I don't know if Swaps could have won the Triple Crown or not. As a guess, maybe he could have beaten Nashua in the Preakness going a mile and three-sixteenths, but I'm not sure he could have gone a good mile and one-half against a top horse like Nashua on a track like Belmont. Swaps never did impress me as a top-distance horse. He was a real good horse, a great one, but only at certain distances. On those sandy, cuppy tracks in the East, against good competition, I'm not sure he could have made the mile and a half. As a four-year-old, in 1956, when he won the Sunset Handicap at Hollywood Park going a mile and five-eighths, he just outclassed his opposition so much that he could do it. He was just so good that I'd get tired holding him, and pretty soon my hands would hurt. And he just kept galloping them to death because he was so superior. But in New York, with a different class of horses, I think a mile and one-quarter was about Swaps' maximum effective distance.

Facing page, left: Horse and rider eye the camera in this unusual picture of Willie Shoemaker at work. —*Michael Gill*

Facing page, right: Shoemaker as he appeared prior to breaking John Longden's record for career winners at Del Mar in 1970.—*Paul Oxley*

Below: Trainer Mish Tenney leads Swaps, with Shoemaker up, out of the saddling paddock at Hollywood Park for a stakes race in 1955.—*Vic Stein & Associates*

Above: Nashua, with Eddie Arcaro up, draws out to a commanding lead in the stretch over Swaps, who is being eased by Willie Shoemaker, in the epic match race at Washington Park in 1955.—*Chicago Tribune*

Right: With Shoemaker in the saddle, Swaps establishes a world's record of 1:33⅕ for one mile in winning the 1956 Argonaut Handicap at Hollywood Park.—*Vic Stein & Associates*

Back in California, right after the Kentucky Derby, Swaps won three stakes pretty easily at Hollywood Park, including a win over older horses in the Californian. In this race, he beat the '54 Derby winner, Determine, by about a length, running the mile and one-sixteenth in 1:40⅖, a new world's record at the time. After he won the Westerner at Hollywood, going a mile and one-quarter, Rex shipped him to Chicago, and we came in first in the American Derby at Washington Park, the only time in his career Swaps won on the grass.

Nashua hadn't been beaten since Swaps did it in the Derby, so there was a natural demand for a match race between them, which was scheduled for August 31, 1955, going a mile and one-quarter, at Washington Park. I was on Swaps, of course, and Eddie rode Nashua. Both horses carried 126 pounds, just like in the Derby. Nashua beat Swaps that day, but I don't think Swaps was right. The starter opened the gate before Swaps was ready, and he came out sideways. It had been raining and the track was drying out, but that track at Washington Park dried out spotty. Some places were dry and other places were still kind of muddy. Well, Eddie popped Nashua out of the gate and got him on that dry path, and I was stuck in the deeper footing. Eddie went right to the lead and was there the whole way. Swaps tried to get to Nashua several times but just couldn't do it. I finally eased Swaps in the stretch when I saw we couldn't win.

Above: Accompanied by trainer Mish Tenney on the pony, Shoemaker takes to the Santa Anita track for a morning workout on stakes star Terrang.—*California Thoroughbred Breeders' Association*

Right: Eased up by Shoemaker in the stretch when victory seemed assured, Swaps, partially hidden, can't withstand the unexpected challenge of Porterhouse and jockey Ismael (Milo) Valenzuela in the controversial 1956 Californian Stakes at Hollywood Park. —*Vic Stein & Associates*

I didn't want to make excuses after the race, but Swaps did have some excuses. Mish and Rex thought about scratching him the night before. I heard later that Swaps could hardly get out of his stall the morning of the race. He had an infection in his right front foot and wore a leather pad to protect it. Mish worked him in the slop the day before, and the dirt got up in there and infected it worse. The next morning, he could hardly walk, and they were considering scratching him and calling the race off. But Ben Lindheimer, who owned Washington Park, said, "You can't do that," because of all the publicity and the money and everything involved. Mish told Harry, "Don't tell Shoe there's anything wrong with Swaps, because he'll pull him up and make a farce out of the race." Actually, I think they thought Swaps could beat Nashua anyway. I didn't know about the infected foot until it was all over. I know Swaps seemed to warm up okay before the race, but it was hard to tell for sure because a lot of the track was muddy. Both horses were laboring in the going, so you couldn't really tell with Swaps whether it was because he was hurting or if it was the racetrack that was causing it.

You can't take anything away from Arcaro's ride on Nashua. He just rode a great race. If I'd drawn inside, where Eddie was, I would have tried to do exactly what he did—pop out of the gate and get to the dry path. Possibly, if Swaps had broken sharp, instead of sideways and veering to the outside, and I had hit him in his ass, then maybe Nashua wouldn't have out-run him to the first turn. Going into the race, I didn't have any strategy. I was just going to lay along with Nashua and see what developed. Eddie had a definite plan, and I knew what he wanted to do all the time.

Most match races are won by the horse who makes the lead. And the reason for that is that it's only a two-horse race and the guy that gets in front can take a hold of his horse and can hold that horse as long as he's not being pressed. When you're laying second in a match race, you have to be the aggressor and move on your horse in order to make the rider on the lead horse move too. You've got to put pressure on him, and that probably puts more pressure on your horse than on the horse in front. The lead horse is in the driver's seat, and you're playing catch-up. Eddie rode a super race, and I'm not too sure if Swaps had been

100 percent that I would have done anything different. And what I did was a mistake. After losing to Nashua in Chicago, Swaps was shipped back home. He had to get that foot taken care of. He was in bad shape for a while with that infected foot.

Everyone said I went to sleep when Swaps got beat by Porterhouse in the 1956 Californian at Hollywood Park. But it really isn't true. Swaps hadn't had a race in about six weeks, and Mish Tenney told me before the race that the colt wasn't as fit as he should be and not to make it a tough race on him if I could help it. And that's how it happened.

Swaps was about three in front at the eighth pole. I was easy-riding him and looked around, and there was no one there. I kept glancing back, and then I heard Porterhouse coming—you can't help hearing a horse coming up on you—and saw him in plenty of time. I chirped to Swaps, trying to get him going, and he just couldn't. Hell, when I was three in front, if I'd gone on with him and kept riding him he probably would have lasted and won. But it might have hurt him too. I had him relaxed to have an easy race, and I couldn't get him going again because he wasn't sharp and he was getting tired. And that's why he got beat that day. Mish took the blame because he told me to do what I did.

I don't know much about the subconscious mind, but it's possible that when Ralph Lowe told me his dream about his rider standing up and misjudging the finish in the 1957 Kentucky Derby, he planted that idea subconsciously. My thinking on it is that I hadn't ridden at Churchill Downs in a year, and my mistake was in not riding a race or two before the Derby to get the feel of the different terrain and the way the track is built and where the finish line is located. I didn't get the mount on Gallant Man until almost the last minute, and I didn't have the chance to line up an earlier mount on the card. Gallant Man had run in the Wood Memorial in New York, and Bold Ruler beat him by a nose. He moved to Bold Ruler and got head and head, maybe a little in front, and Bold Ruler came back and hung it on him. John Choquette, the jock who had been riding Gallant Man and was going to ride him in the Kentucky Derby, was suspended, so Johnny Nerud, the colt's trainer, called and asked me to ride Gallant Man in the Derby.

I got into Louisville Friday night before the Derby, and Mr. Lowe, Nerud, and myself had dinner together. That's when Lowe told me his dream about the jock who rode his horse misjudging the finish. I said, "Oh, Mr. Lowe, don't worry about that. It's never going to happen to me. I've ridden in this race too many times. It's not going to happen." The next day it happened. I couldn't believe it after it was all over. I thought that never could happen to me because I thought I couldn't do anything wrong. At that stage of my career, I just thought I did everything right all the time. I wasn't cocky about it. I just had that feeling inside. But it did happen, and it really set me back a little bit. I said to myself, "Well, you're not as good as you think you are. You can make a mistake once in a while too, like everybody else." As it turned out, that experience really did help me.

Most of the riders in the jocks' room and the guys who rode in the race knew I'd stood up, I suppose. It had happened before at Churchill Downs, but not in the Derby and not for the win. It happened many times with guys in different races. At Churchill Downs, the finish is about a sixteenth of a mile farther up the track, closer to the clubhouse turn, than at tracks where I'd been riding—and riding hard I just blew it. After my goof, Churchill Downs put up a big bull's-eye over the finish to make sure all the jocks knew where the line was.

Right: Momentarily confused, Willie Shoemaker on Gallant Man misjudges the finish line and stands up in the irons at the sixteenth pole while fighting for the lead with Calumet Farm's Iron Liege, ridden by Bill Hartack, in the 1957 Kentucky Derby. Realizing his error instantly, Shoemaker sits back down to ride out the Ralph Lowe-owned colt but is unable to overhaul Iron Liege, losing by a nose.—*UPI*

Below: Gallant Man (5) and Shoemaker fail to catch Iron Liege, ridden by Bill Hartack, by the slim margin of a nose after Shoemaker misjudged the finish line and stood up in the stirrups in the 1957 Kentucky Derby.—*Caufield & Shook, Inc.*

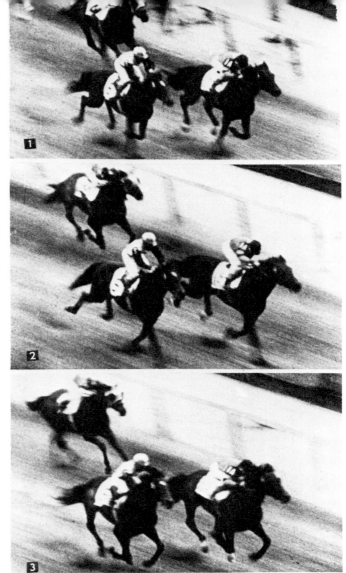

Led by trainer Bill Molter, the Travis Kerr-owned colt and stakes star Bobby Brocato and Shoemaker are en route to the Hollywood Park track for a morning workout in 1957. Molter also developed Round Table.—*Vic Stein & Associates*

I don't think I ever made the lead in that Derby. I was close, but I never did get to the front of Iron Liege, the Calumet Farm horse Bill Hartack was riding. I thought the race was over and I'd lost when I stood up. Eventually, the winning margin was a nose, which was as close as I got to Iron Liege.

Gallant Man was the kind of horse who'd relax when you stood up on him after the finish, but I'm not sure he relaxed that day. He was trying hard before we got there and was really starting to hang just a little bit. I wasn't too sure I was going to win it even before I stood up. Of course, it would be silly now for me to say I wouldn't have won it anyway. That would be like defending what I did, and I've never done that. The truth is I really don't know whether my mistake made him lose the race or not.

After the race, one of the stewards called me on the phone and asked, "What happened?" I hesitated for a couple of seconds, and then I said, "I made a mistake, I misjudged the finish line." I considered briefly telling him a story, but I realized that would have been silly. I felt bad about my mistake, for Mr. Lowe, but he took it well and was very nice about it. The stewards said, "We feel the same way you do. We think you made an honest mistake, and we're not going to take any action because of that."

I went to Dallas, and the next day I received a telegram from the stewards in Louisville saying, "Under the circumstances, we are compelled to inform you we have suspended you for 15 days." I didn't appreciate the way they did it. I guess they got to thinking about it and talking and decided they'd better take some action, for the public, which I didn't mind. I should have been suspended, but I didn't like the way they did it. What I had done wasn't deliberate. It was an honest mistake. But you shouldn't make such a serious mistake if you're a professional rider. So they were entitled to take some action, and they did. Ralph Lowe felt bad for me and mad because the stewards set me down for 15 days. And he wouldn't run Gallant Man in the Preakness because of that. He sent me a new Chrysler. I don't know, maybe he felt this was going to affect my career, although he never told me that.

But I really felt bad about it. What the hell, Gallant Man had a chance to win and he didn't win. Then I decided I'd made a mistake, I'd made some mistakes before, and I'd probably make more before I was through. And if I let this one affect me, it was going to affect my career, and I just wasn't going to let that happen. I was going to go on from there. You get beat in a race sometimes when you think you should have won, and it eats some guys up.

Right: Shoemaker accepts award from Santa Anita executives Leigh M. Battson, right, and Carleton F. Burke after recording the 3,000th winner of his career in 1958. Mrs. Ginny Shoemaker joins in the ceremony.—*Vic Stein & Associates*

Below: In 1958, officials of Hollywood Park unveiled a life-sized statue of Swaps with Shoemaker in his familiar pose atop the "California Comet."—*Vic Stein & Associates*

They worry about it and think about it and get mad, and they're going to mess up in the next race worrying over a race that's already gone. And this is something you can't afford to do. You've got to tell yourself, "Sorry it happened. I feel bad about it, but I'm not going to worry about it. It's done, and I can't go back and do it over again. I can't do anything about it, and I'm not going to let it bother me that much." And that's the way I looked at it. It was a real test of my mental discipline, but I'd always recognized it as a weakness when I saw riders get mad about losing a race and then go out and ride a bad race because they didn't give a damn. They're going to feel bad about this one too later on. I don't think I ever fell into that trap. When I made a mistake, it wasn't because I was thinking about some race I lost— and maybe should have won—earlier in the day.

After the Derby, I think the public sympathized with me. I was the underdog, and the public loves an underdog. People always like to see the underdog prevail and come through and win. I'd been on the other side most of my life, and when you're not the underdog, they boo you when you get beat on the favorites. It's all right. I don't mind. They pay their money to come in and watch you. They bet their money on your horse and they lose. They're entitled to holler and scream and boo, or whatever else they want to do within reason. I'd probably do the same thing if I were back there betting. I was needled a lot by the fans when I came back after the 15-day suspension. Guys would say, "Hey, the finish line's over here, Shoe, don't forget now where it is." But that kind of thing is going to happen. It's part of the game, and you don't let it bother you.

Mr. Lowe entered Gallant Man in the Belmont, and I went back to ride him. Gallant Man ran one of his greatest races that day, winning by eight lengths in the American-record time of 2:26⅗ for a mile and one-half. Bold Ruler, with Arcaro up, was in the field after taking the Preakness, and Gallant Man just breezed by him at the top of the stretch and went on from there.

I got my 3,000th victory early in 1958 and finished up the year leading rider, with 300 winners. The nearly $3 million in earnings by my mounts was also tops. This was the year I rode Silky Sullivan, a colt from California who got a lot of publicity beating mediocre horses at Santa Anita by coming from far out of it and getting up to win. But there was no way he was going to spot a good horse like Calumet Farm's Tim Tam that many lengths, and he was up the track, 12th, and about 20 lengths behind Tim Tam in the Kentucky Derby.

Although not at his absolute best, Gallant Man still was good enough under Shoemaker's direction to capture the 1958 Hollywood Gold Cup, beating Eddie Schmidt.—*Author's Collection*

Tomy Lee, right foreground, with Shoemaker in the saddle, is second coming down the stretch, but edged out Sword Dancer, ridden by Bill Boland, to capture the 1959 Kentucky Derby.—*Wide World*

A Bump in Time

I N 1959, Elliott Burch, one of the top trainers in the East, called me to ride Sword Dancer in the Stepping Stone before the Kentucky Derby. Sword Dancer won, and I was very impressed with him and wanted to ride him in the Derby. In the meantime, Harry Silbert had told Frank Childs, who trained Tomy Lee, that if his colt won with me in the Blue Grass Stakes at Keeneland, I would ride him in the Derby. So Tomy Lee won the Blue Grass, and I had to stick with the commitment. I wanted to ride Sword Dancer but couldn't, and I was disappointed. I told Harry, "We're going to ride Tomy Lee, but Sword Dancer is going to win the Derby." And Harry said, "Well, that's the way it is." Frank Childs was such a nice guy, you couldn't go back on your word. When he told you he'd do something, he'd do it, so you had to be the same way with him.

Of course, I won the race on Tomy Lee, but I don't think I should have. I don't think Bill Boland, who rode Sword Dancer, believes I should have won either. I'm not knocking Billy. He was a great rider, but he made a mistake that day. Tomy Lee used to run out all the time, and Boland thought I was trying to do something to him when Tomy Lee bore out and bumped Sword Dancer. Boland thought I was doing it intentionally, so he'd give it to me right back. But I really wasn't. Boland kept coming back into me through the lane. Only he didn't hurt me, he helped me, because when he bumped Tomy Lee, the colt switched from his left lead to his right lead, giving him the energy to come on and beat Sword Dancer by a nose. Had Boland gotten away from me and gone on about his business, I believe Sword Dancer would have won. After we went around the first turn, Tomy Lee got on his left lead and stayed on it all the way into the stretch, until Sword Dancer bumped him and made him switch.

I remember Tomy Lee the year before the Derby. First Landing was the top two-year-old, but the only reason he beat Tomy Lee in the Garden State Stakes was that Tomy Lee didn't make the first turn. We were in number-ten post position, and it was a sloppy track. Tomy Lee was running out all the way, and I had to fight him like hell. He was in the middle of the racetrack all the way around the first turn. I finally got him to switch his lead and got him in to the rail, but all that wrestling around took enough out of him for First Landing to win by a neck. Had Tomy Lee gone around that first turn the way a horse normally would, relaxed and kind, he would have beaten First Landing a couple of lengths. But I never was impressed with Tomy Lee as a distance horse. Sword Dancer was a true distance horse and better qualified to go the mile and one-quarter of the Kentucky Derby than Tomy Lee.

Left: Surrounded by the sweet smell of success, Shoemaker and roses-bedraped Tomy Lee take their stance in the winner's circle after defeating Sword Dancer in the 1959 Kentucky Derby. At Tomy Lee's head is the colt's owner, Fred Turner, while trainer Frank Childs is at left.—*Caufield & Shook, Inc.*

Below: Sword Dancer and jockey Willie Shoemaker, a winning team in the Belmont Stakes in 1959, combine to capture the Monmouth Handicap in impressive style. Sword Dancer went on to become Horse of the Year in '59.—*Wide World*

69

After the Derby, I went to ride Sword Dancer in the Preakness. Tomy Lee was running the same day at Hollywood Park in the Cinema Handicap. Fred Turner, Tomy Lee's owner, got mad because I didn't ride his horse. But I liked Sword Dancer better all the time. Don Pierce rode Tomy Lee, and the colt went around the first turn running out, over horses' heels, and he got beat. That made Turner even angrier. He didn't think Tomy Lee should have lost, but I thought he would have been beaten anyway. Tomy Lee was lucky to win the Derby, in my opinion. After the Derby, Turner had said, "Well, the bookmakers had Shoemaker, and the horse won in spite of Shoemaker." That's what he said. You know he had to be an ass to say something like that, because I was riding my fanny off to try and win the race. Anybody with any knowledge of racing could see that. If I had been trying to hold the horse, it would have been obvious. So he made an ass out of himself with that ridiculous statement.

Sword Dancer couldn't handle Royal Orbit in the Preakness, and we were decisively beaten, by four lengths. Bill Harmatz was the winning jock. But Sword Dancer showed his real distance ability in the Belmont Stakes, when he defeated Bagdad, ridden by Bobby Ussery, by three-quarters of a length.

It turned out to be another good year for me. In addition to winning the Derby and the Belmont in 1959, I ended up the leader both in winners, with 347, and in earnings won by my mounts, with more than $2.8 million. It also was the year I was elected to the Jockeys' Hall of Fame at Pimlico, and that was an honor I felt pretty good about receiving.

In May of '61, at Hollywood Park, a couple of weeks after I'd come back from the Kentucky Derby—where I was fourth on Dr. Miller behind Carry Back with John Sellers riding—I picked up my 4,000th winner, on a horse named Guaranteeya. Only three other jocks had ridden more winners up to that time: Longden, Arcaro, and Sir Gordon Richards of England.

Left: Aboard Guaranteeya in the third race at Hollywood Park on May 19, 1961, Willie Shoemaker records the 4,000th victory of his career. Previously, only John Longden, Eddie Arcaro, and England's Sir Gordon Richards had accomplished the feat.—*Wide World*

Right: "The Shoe" applies his magic touch to harness racing in an exhibition at Santa Anita in the early '60s. —*Author's Collection*

Below: Crimson Satan and Shoemaker gallop away with a winner's prize of $180,819 in the 1961 Garden State Stakes at Garden State Park in New Jersey. Only a nose separated the second- and third-place horses—Donut King, with Don Pierce in the saddle, and Obey, with Howard Grant up.—*Author's Collection*

Riding a race which he considers among the best of his career, Shoemaker masterfully keeps Olden Times in front for approximately a mile and three-quarters and wins the San Juan Capistrano Handicap in 1962 at Santa Anita. Olden Times won many stakes races with "The Shoe" in the saddle.—*Author's Collection*

Jaipur, a Nasrullah colt owned by George D. Widener, gave me my third win in the Belmont Stakes in 1962. Jaipur wasn't the easiest horse in the world to ride, and he just did nose out Admiral's Voyage, whose jock was Braulio Baeza.

The Preakness was the one Triple Crown race I hadn't been able to win until 1963, when Candy Spots beat Chateaugay, who had finished first in the Kentucky Derby with Baeza in the saddle. Candy Spots, the favorite in both races, won the Preakness by 3½ lengths but was third in the Derby. Chateaugay probably was the best colt sired by Swaps, and he beat us again in the Belmont Stakes a few weeks later. The Belmont was run at Aqueduct that year because the old grandstand at Belmont Park wasn't considered safe anymore and they were rebuilding it. Candy Spots, who was owned by Rex Ellsworth, was a good horse for me in 1963, winning six stakes races, all hundred-granders.

76   *The SHOE*

Left top: Victory in his third Belmont Stakes was Shoemaker's when Jaipur just barely managed to nose out the tenacious Admiral's Voyage, with Braulio Baeza up, in the 1962 running of the mile and one-half classic. Crimson Satan was third. Left bottom: Jaipur and Shoemaker head for the winner's circle.—*Author's Collection*

Below: Shoemaker wins the 1962 Mother Goose Stakes at Belmont Park aboard Cicada, "a tough little filly." Cicada and "The Shoe" combined to win ten stakes races.—*Author's Collection*

Left: Sitting chilly, Shoemaker guides talented Never Bend to a handy triumph over Outing Class, with Don Pierce up, in the $152,000 Futurity for two-year-olds at Aqueduct in 1962.—*Wide World*

Below: Jaipur responds to the right-hand whip of Shoemaker to shade Ridan, ridden by Manuel Ycaza, in the 1962 running of the Travers Stakes at Saratoga. Military Plume (left), with John Sellers up, was third. —*Wide World*

Above: A winner of six races on a single program several times during his career, "The Shoe" turned the trick for the first time at Santa Anita on February 23, 1962. Congratulating him is Clerk of Scales Hubert S. Jones, who as an apprentice rider in 1944 at Agua Caliente won with eight of 13 mounts on the program.—*Vic Stein & Associates*

Left: With sportscaster Chris Schenkel in the background, Shoemaker receives a victory kiss from his second wife, Babbs, after winning his first Preakness Stakes, on Candy Spots in 1963.—*Jerry Cooke/Sports Illustrated*

Right: Champions eye each other in 1964 at Hollywood Park, where Shoemaker is watching five-time Horse of the Year Kelso being cooled out on the tow ring in the stable area.—*Vic Stein & Associates*

For the '64 Kentucky Derby, I had my choice of Northern Dancer, a Canadian-bred colt I'd won the Florida Derby on, and George Pope's Hill Rise, a California colt who won the Santa Anita Derby with Don Pierce. I figured Hill Rise was a better horse than Northern Dancer, so I went for him. But there was another reason I chose Hill Rise.

The Scoundrel, who was owned by Ellsworth and trained by Mish Tenney, was second to Northern Dancer in the Florida Derby, and I was getting some pressure to ride him in Kentucky. Rex and Mish figured The Scoundrel could beat Northern Dancer the next time they hooked up. They really didn't want me on Northern Dancer in the Derby, but they said, "If you can ride Hill Rise in the Derby, go ahead, because we think he's the best three-year-old around. But if you can't, then we'd like you to be on The Scoundrel and not Northern Dancer."

So I went for Hill Rise, because I thought he was the best colt too. Bill Hartack picked up Northern Dancer, and they beat us by a neck in the Derby. But I had some trouble in the race, including being bumped twice, and Hill Rise might have been the best horse in the race after all.

Earlier in 1964, at Santa Anita, I got home on a horse owned by Ellsworth and trained by Tenney and went past Arcaro's all-time earnings record of more than $30 million. In October, I got my 5,000th winner at Aqueduct back in New York. Longden was the only other rider to have won 5,000, so I joined him in pretty exclusive company. The horse's name was Slapstick, and I remember he won handily going seven-eighths. For the tenth time—and the seventh in a row—I was leading rider in total purses for the year.

Below: "The Shoe" chalks up his 5,000th career winner, aboard Slapstick in the fifth race at Aqueduct on October 22, 1964, joining John Longden as the only rider in history to win as many races.—*Author's Collection*

Right: Willie was awarded a gold clock to commemorate his 5,000th winner.—*Wide World*

Above: When John Longden retired as a jockey in 1966 and turned his talents to conditioning Thoroughbreds, he chose friend Willie Shoemaker to ride his first entrant, and they proved to be a winning combination as Attention III scored at Hollywood Park.—*Wide World*

Right top: "The Shoe" parades to the post aboard Royal Derby II (4) for the fifth race at Santa Anita on March 14, 1976. Due to the special circumstances —Willie's try for his 7,000th victory—Royal Derby was the 3-to-1 favorite in the mile and one-eighth turf event, even though he hadn't won a race in almost three years.—*Michael Gill*

Right bottom: Shoemaker and Chilean-bred stretch-runner Cougar II, popularly known as the "Big Cat," were a formidable combination, winning 11 stakes races.—*Allen W. Hopkins*

Overleaf following: Cougar II and Shoemaker capture the classic San Juan Capistrano Handicap in 1971. Fort Marcy, with Jorge Velasquez up, was second, but was disqualified.—*Vic Stein & Associates*

I won my third Kentucky Derby in '65 on Lucky Debonair, a game three-year-old owned by Ada L. Rice and trained by Frank Catrone. We barely held on to beat Dapper Dan, ridden by Milo Valenzuela. Tom Rolfe came in third, but it's possible he was best that day. Ron Turcotte, who was riding Tom Rolfe, tried to get through on the inside around the last turn. Flag Raiser, with Bobby Ussery up, was on the lead, and I was laying second on Lucky Debonair. Ussery saw Turcotte trying to get through and closed the door on him. Turcotte had to take back and come around, and Tom Rolfe never could make up that much ground.

Left top: En route to earning acclaim as champion three-year-old filly of 1971, Turkish Trousers, ridden by "The Shoe," wins the Hollywood Oaks. Convenience, with Jerry Lambert in the saddle, was second.—*Vic Stein & Associates*

Left bottom: Shoemaker wins his 100th hundred-grander race, aboard Miss Musket in the 1974 Fantasy Stakes at Oaklawn Park.—*Tibor Abahazy*

Above: Exhorted to an all-out effort by Shoemaker, Lucky Debonair is fairly flying with all four feet off the ground en route to winning the 1965 Kentucky Derby. Dapper Dan, with Milo Valenzuela riding, was second; Tom Rolfe, with Ron Turcotte, third. It was Shoemaker's third triumph in the "Run for the Roses."—*Robert Kingsbury*

Above: Shoemaker holds the roses in the Churchill Downs winner's circle after his triumph on Lucky Debonair in the '65 Kentucky Derby.—*Caufield & Shook, Inc.*

Right: Shoemaker answers sportswriters' questions in the Churchill Downs jockeys' room after winning the Kentucky Derby astride Lucky Debonair.—*Wide World*

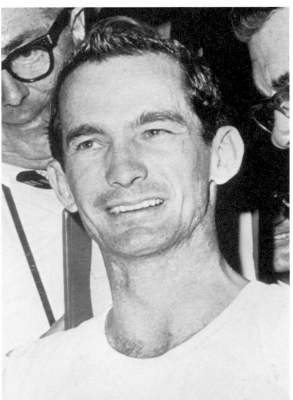

I remember that just a few days before Lucky Debonair's Derby, on a bet, I worked a horse in the morning, in the dark, at about five o'clock. I was wearing a tuxedo and a top coat, and a friend of mine dared me to do it. So there I was, working this horse five-eighths in my dinner jacket, just for kicks.

The odds were 8–5 on Lucky Debonair in the Preakness, but he hurt himself in the race and finished seventh to Tom Rolfe. Lucky Debonair was out until early in 1966, and he came back to win the Santa Anita Handicap. In fact, he was the only horse to win the Santa Anita Derby, the Kentucky Derby, and the Santa Anita Handicap—three pretty good races.

Tom Rolfe and Shoemaker had little difficulty winning the Chicagoan Stakes in 1965 at Arlington Park. The Preakness Stakes winner, Tom Rolfe was shipped to France later in the year to run in the Prix de l'Arc de Triomphe.—*Author's Collection*

The SHOE

Left: On hand at Longchamp racecourse outside Paris, France, prior to the 1965 Arc de Triomphe were Willie Shoemaker, who rode American invader Tom Rolfe, and Bing Crosby, owner of Meadow Court, another entrant in Europe's richest race. Tom Rolfe finished sixth to Sea Bird II.—*Wide World*

Below: Dr. Fager, a colt of brilliance trained by Johnny Nerud, wins the Cowdin Stakes for two-year-olds under Shoemaker in 1966.—*Author's Collection*

Late in 1966, I was riding back in New York and I started getting up in the morning on a colt named Damascus, trained by Frank Whiteley, who also had Tom Rolfe in the barn. Whiteley thought Damascus had all the makings of a really good horse, and he sure was right. I won ten stakes races on Damascus in '67, and seven of them were hundred-granders. He didn't run his race in the Kentucky Derby, and we were third to Proud Clarion, with Bobby Ussery riding. After that Damascus won everything in sight—the Preakness, the Belmont, and he cinched out Horse of the Year when he beat Dr. Fager and Buckpasser in the Woodward Stakes by ten lengths. Damascus, who was owned by Mrs. Edith W. Bancroft, had some year. He won $817,941, and that was a record for one year.

Damascus and "The Shoe" have a fairly easy time of it in winning the 1967 Belmont Stakes (left and below). In second place was Cool Reception, with John Sellers aboard. Gentleman James, with Jimmy Nichols riding, finished third. Damascus provided Shoemaker with his fourth Belmont Stakes success and went on to earn Horse of the Year acclaim. Horse and rider had also captured the Preakness, but were third in the Kentucky Derby.—*Author's Collection*

Confined to bed at Daniel Freeman Hospital with the first major injury of his career, a broken leg sustained in the spill at Santa Anita in 1968, Shoemaker admires a bouquet of flowers studded with pari-mutuel tickets sent to him by friends. Sister Mary Esther, hospital administrator, helps him hold the bouquet.—*Wide World*

"Sometimes You Fall"

I HAD A LOT OF spills over the years, but I was lucky I didn't get hurt many times. Any time you fall, if you can ball-up and roll when you hit the ground, and have time to do it, fine. That's an instinct maybe I had. But sometimes you fall and don't have time to protect yourself. You have to be lucky. Many years ago, I rode a filly named Dutch Wife, who was trained by Buster Millerick. Going seven-eighths, I was in the number-one post position, and I'm on the lead about a half-length coming down there in the first sixteenth of a mile, and I'm clocking the field to the outside. Well, she got to the gap leading to the track where the horses walk through, and she just turned left while I'm looking the other way. I went off, hit the track, and rolled underneath the rail. She hit a support post, and we wound up together on the other side of the fence. That was luck, how could it be anything else? I missed the support post and wound up right on her belly, in between her legs. She broke her neck, and it killed her. She already was dead, or she might have kicked me.

That spill in the 1963 Santa Anita Derby when I was on Candy Spots is another example of luck. Going around the first turn, I was in behind the first bunch of horses. There were four or five in front of me, and I wasn't too far in behind them. Henry Moreno was on a horse called Tourlourou, and as he began to move up, his horse started to bolt and hit me, knocking me to the outside about two horses farther out than I would have been. At the same time, Milo Valenzuela's horse, Win-Em-All, clipped the heels of his stablemate, Sky Gem, and went down. Three other horses went down too. I missed it only because Moreno's colt came out and knocked me out of the way, otherwise I would have gone right over the top of them. That shows you fate and the luck in the running of a race. And I wound up winning the race on Candy Spots. From a disaster to a victory, that's pure luck, really.

It takes most riders a little while to put a spill out of their minds. You're bound to think about it, like that Dutch Wife spill I took. Sometimes you're edgy for a while. Most guys are—those that have any common sense, that is. But after you ride a few races, you get your confidence back again. I had three horses break their legs with me in one day at Santa Anita. Luckily, I got them all pulled up without going down. But you're thinking, "Well, Jesus Christ, what's going to happen next?" And you ask yourself, "If I let him run and bow down and ride him hard, is he going to do the same thing?"

You don't really think about falling until the first time it happens. Once you realize it can happen, you think about falling in a different context than you did when you first started and didn't know what it was to be in a spill. Every time you go by the place where you fell, you're ready for anything. You don't want it to happen again so you prepare and correct for it if a situation comes up. That's just being cautious and taking preventive measures. You can't be overcautious, but you still must use common sense. You don't move up into a hole unless you know you have enough horse to get you in there in the right position. You don't drive into a spot just inching up to it like you did when you first began to ride.

In the early days, I used to gallop an old mare named Gallahue for George Reeves. She wasn't too tough, but every day at one spot she'd prop and go the other way and I'd go off. And every time I was ready for her. I'd say, "Well, you're not going to get me today." And every time she'd get me. She wouldn't run off then, she'd just stay in one spot and look at me, as if to say, "You dumb son of a bitch, I got you again, didn't I?" She could either gallop very nice, or she could get on the bit and run off with you. One morning at the old Tanforan track, I was galloping her and she ran off. This was like from the three-eighths pole to the quarter pole, and she's running off with me and running out and I'm trying to shake the bit in her mouth and change her mind. Well, I got off-balance and fell off on the left side and landed right on my back in the middle of the racetrack.

Left top: His crutches close at hand, Willie recovers at home from the broken leg he suffered in 1968. —*Sheedy & Long/Sports Illustrated*

Left bottom: Still on crutches while recuperating from a broken leg, Shoemaker studies the Hollywood Park program with wife Babbs and jockey Laffit Pincay.—*Vic Stein & Associates*

Overleaf: The pictures, blown up to show as much detail as possible, are from the official patrol films of the January 23, 1968, race at Santa Anita in which Shoemaker suffered his first major injury. Top left: Seeing apprentice Juan Gonzalez as he is spilled from the falling Kodiak Kid, Shoemaker (arrow), on Bel Bush, realizes he can't avoid an accident and prepares himself for impending disaster. Bottom left: The champion rider and his horse are down. Kodiak Kid, left, and Bel Bush struggle to regain their feet as Shoemaker (in white and obscured by tree in foreground) lies stunned on the ground. Top right: As Bel Bush rises, he strikes Shoemaker with a hind leg, breaking the femur bone of the jockey's right leg. Bottom right: With Kodiak Kid trapped under the rail, Bel Bush takes off in pursuit of the field. When he came to, "I knew my leg was broken," said Shoemaker later. Gonzalez escaped without serious injury, but was killed in a racing spill in 1975 at Pleasanton, California.

I just laid there on the track for about ten or 15 minutes, and guys were galloping by and I couldn't get up. I was paralyzed from the waist down. I don't know if they even had ambulances around on the track. Finally, the feeling started coming back in my legs, and I got up and went back to the barn. My back hurt, but I figured it was going to hurt because that's where I landed, and so I didn't go to the doctor. Years later, I fell off leaving the gate one day, just before going East to ride Swaps in the Derby. I went to the hospital for X rays, and the doctor said, "You broke a vertebra in your back." "Are you kidding?" I said. "But it looks like an old injury, it looks like it's a few years old. It's healed. Sometime in your life, you chipped a vertebra in your back." And that was the time Gallahue dropped me. She was a temperamental old bitch, but I won a ton of races on her.

When you're going good and riding good horses and winning races, everything seems to flow right and work well. Early in 1968, I won two stakes races on Damascus, and he looked like a lock in the $100,000 Strub Stakes [formerly the Santa Anita Maturity] coming up two weeks later. Then it all came apart. On January 23, at Santa Anita, I had a fall and broke my right leg, and I was laid up for more than a year. It was the first time I was hurt bad enough to be laid up that long. The most it had ever been before was two or three weeks.

I was in the middle of the pack on Bel Bush, and Don Pierce was right outside of me on a horse called Top Floor. Watching up ahead, I saw Juan Gonzalez, a bug boy on a horse named Kodiak Kid, going for a spot he shouldn't be going for. And I yelled, "Hey, don't, don't do that! Don't go in there, jock!" Pierce said, "What?" "Look at that jock," I said to Pierce. "Don't go in there, don't go in there!" I yelled again. Pierce happened to be looking to the outside, and by the time he looked around my way, Gonzalez was down. Had Pierce

Left: Instrumental in Shoemaker's recovery from a broken leg was his close friend Dr. Robert Kerlan, a leading orthopedic specialist and surgeon.—*Wide World*

Right: On the mend from a broken leg suffered in January, Shoemaker, along with Hall-of-Fame trainer Bill Winfrey, right, visited American troops stationed in Vietnam in September of 1968.—*Author's Collection*

been looking inside, he would have wheeled out and maybe I could have ducked out. But he was looking outside, and by the time he came back my way Kodiak Kid had clipped the heels of the horse in front of him and was down. Pierce saw it then and wheeled out, but it was too late for me. I caught that horse's ass and went down too. I saw it coming long before it happened, but I couldn't get out. Gonzalez had tried to go between two horses where he had no business being. There wasn't enough room. I'm not knocking him, because he had the bug at the time, and it was something any apprentice might do. Anyway, I went right off my horse, and when he started to get up he hit me with a hind leg and busted the femur of my right leg. I was knocked out for a few seconds. When I woke up, I tried to move, and I knew my leg was broken. The pain wasn't that bad, but it did hurt a little.

Dr. Robert Kerlan, a good friend of mine and one of the top orthopedic men in the United States, operated on me and inserted a metal pin in the middle of the bone, extending from the hip through the thigh, to help it knit properly. I was in the hospital about three weeks. The time at home in the beginning was tough because I couldn't do anything. I had to lay there and couldn't get around, and I nearly went crazy for about a month, until I got used to the convalescence part of it. Because the femur is the largest bone in your body, it takes the longest to heal. Mine took such a long time to knit that Dr. Kerlan was considering a bone graft. But it finally mended.

After a period of six or seven months, I had some doubts about being able to ride again. Because of the lack of activity, the muscles in my leg had deteriorated, and the leg was all withered up. It was about as big around as a silver dollar at one time. I said to myself, "No way it'll ever come back." But I did a lot of therapy, which was very boring, and after

The SHOE

many hours of lifting weights and walking and bicycling and all, it came back. Now my right leg is an inch bigger than the left because of all the therapy. Then when I started in galloping ponies and exercising horses in the morning, I was stiff all over because of the inactivity. My right knee was so stiff that I could barely bend it, and I had to work like hell to finally get it to operate. While I was recovering, the leg was held out straight and the knee lost its elasticity and mobility. It took a long time to regain that too.

Even though I felt I was fit enough to start riding again, I was apprehensive. Thirteen months is a long time to be laid up. You tend to get flabby, your muscles deteriorate, and you don't know if you can do the things you did before. I had more self-doubt during this period than at any time in my life. But I've always been a fatalist, and I figured, "I'm going to see if I can cut it. If I can't, then I can't, and I'll quit. I'm going to give it a good try. What the hell, why be nervous? Either you can do it or you can't. If you can't, then quit like you should. So what?" And that was the way I felt about it.

I made my comeback at Santa Anita on February 11, 1969, and it's one date I'll never forget. I was riding in three races that afternoon, and I won my first one, on a filly named Princess Endeavour. The crowd gave me a big ovation, and that really made me feel good. In the eighth race, the feature, I was on Racing Room, and we beat the favorite, Tumiga, by more than a length and tied the track record for 6½ furlongs while we were at it. I rode Jay's Double in the ninth race. This one was close all the way, but I won it too. The Good Lord was looking out for me when I won my first day back. It was good horses and faith.

Below: Back in the saddle after 13 months on the sidelines recovering from a broken right leg, Shoemaker appears deadly serious as he goes to the track on his first comeback mount, Princess Endeavour, February 11, 1969, at Santa Anita.—*Sheedy & Long/Sports Illustrated*

Right: Shoemaker has Princess Endeavour under stout restraint as he saves the filly for an all-out effort in the stretch.—*Sheedy & Long/Sports Illustrated*

108   *The SHOE*

Left: Head down and driving toward the wire, Shoemaker launches his comeback with a victory astride Princess Endeavour.—*Herb Shoebridge*

Above: A winner with his first mount in 13 months, Shoemaker poses atop Princess Endeavour in the Santa Anita victory enclosure.—*Sheedy & Long/ Sports Illustrated*

Right: Shoemaker makes it two-for-two on the first day of his comeback by guiding Racing Room to victory over favored Tumiga, ridden by Walter Blum. Racing Room ran the 6½ furlongs in 1:15 flat, equaling the track record.—*Herb Shoebridge*

Overleaf following: Obviously inspired, Shoemaker climaxes a perfect afternoon by calling on all his skill to ride Jay's Double to victory over So He Does. Three mounts, three wins—and the world knows that "The Shoe" is back.—*Herb Shoebridge*

That night when I went home, I was really emotional and I cried about winning those three races. The time off had made me appreciate my career and what I had. But I didn't know I enjoyed riding so much or that I would miss it as much as I did when I couldn't do it. You get blasé when you're doing well year after year. Then you have a setback, and you realize you have no business being blasé. You're damned fortunate to be able to do what you enjoy doing. You take things for granted, and when they're taken away, it makes a helluva difference in your attitude. As it turns out, it's possible that spill prolonged my career because it made me realize how much I loved riding horses.

Winning those races my first day back on the track naturally built up my confidence, but I found out I was nowhere near ready, physically or any other way. But it helped my mental attitude. It made me go on trying to get back in shape, and that took about two to three more months. I kept on riding and won a half-dozen or so stakes races during that time.

A couple of months after I was back riding again, Elliott Burch, who had trained Sword Dancer and other top horses, asked me to come to Florida to ride Arts and Letters, a Ribot colt owned by Paul Mellon, in the Florida Derby at Gulfstream Park. Arts and Letters ran a pretty good race but was second to Top Knight, beaten about five lengths. I'd ridden the colt that one time and had the feel of him. Then I went to Keeneland for the Blue Grass, and I rode him differently. I let him roll more the first part of it and didn't take too much hold because he was a funny horse to ride. He wanted to do his own thing. In the Blue Grass I had a hold of him around the first turn, and he was fighting for his head. I let him run then, and he opened up four or five lengths real quick and went on to win by 15. So I felt I'd found out how he liked to run. I thought he had a great chance to win the Kentucky Derby.

A couple of days before the Derby, a filly named Poona's Day flipped over backwards on me in the paddock at Hollywood Park and broke my pelvis and ruptured my bladder. That was the end of my dreams of winning the Derby that year. Arts and Letters ran a helluva race in the Derby—he only got beat a neck by Majestic Prince. Braulio Baeza rode Arts and Letters, and I don't think I would have ridden him much differently. Maybe I would have let him run a little more in the beginning of the race than Baeza did, because I knew the horse that way.

Left: Shoemaker takes Arts and Letters to the winner's circle at Keeneland after the 1969 Blue Grass Stakes, a major stepping-stone to the Kentucky Derby. Arts and Letters crossed the wire 15 lengths in front.—*Louisville Courier-Journal*

Right: Seriously hurt with a fractured pelvis and internal injuries, Shoemaker lies in a heap on the ground in the saddling paddock at Hollywood Park after he was pinned beneath the filly Poona's Day in a freak accident on April 30, 1969. The mishap occurred only a few days before "The Shoe" was scheduled to ride Arts and Letters in the Kentucky Derby. —*California Thoroughbred Breeders' Association*

The pain when I got kicked in the leg was nothing compared to the pain when I got sat on by that filly. My pelvis was broken in five places, my bladder was ruptured, and whatever else it did, that was enough. As it was, I was out about three months. Those injuries heal a lot faster than a broken femur bone, and that's why I was able to come back so much faster this time. The femur takes at least six months to heal, but usually it's anywhere from eight to 12 months.

I didn't lose consciousness when that filly sat on me. I saw stars for a minute, but that was all. I knew she was a fidgety filly, and actually I mostly blame the groom for what happened. If he had turned her loose, she might not have flipped. He was hanging on to her tight, and when she flipped over backwards, he went right over with us. He didn't even turn loose then. You never hold onto horses like that. You turn them loose and let them go, and they'll stop trying to flip.

I felt her getting ready to do it and I was going to get off, but Lou Glauburg, the trainer, was trying to help me and he kind of pushed me back. It happened so fast. I could feel her tighten up when he put me on, and I was getting ready to slide off the left side. Lou felt I wasn't getting on or was slipping off, and he had a hold of my leg and pushed me back on about the time she started to flip. I was off-balance and I just went over, and she landed on top of me.

Because of the internal injuries, I was really sick for a while. I couldn't do anything. I had to lay still and couldn't move, and I had tubes sticking out of my stomach and a catheter in my penis. Oh, it was awful. I thought, "Damn, I don't think I'll ever get on another horse again as long as I live." That's how bad I felt. This one was 20 times worse than the broken leg. When I got home from the hospital, I was on crutches. I walked by the mirror in one of the bedrooms and took a look at my lower body. Both of my legs were really shrunken, and I thought, "Oh my God, I'll never be able to get them back in shape again. No way." And if you'd seen me then, you'd have said, "Never no way will he get back in shape again." Every time I looked I'd think, "Oh, hell, I'll never make it this time."

But it's amazing what nature does for you once you get active again and how fast muscles recuperate and come back. You do the therapy and every day you feel better, and the more exercise you do the stronger you get. Then the muscles start popping out again, and you forget about the hurt and what happened. Nature has a great way of taking care of your mind too. You feel good just to be walking around and being able to do the everyday things you took for granted.

This time it was nothing like coming back after the broken leg. There was no doubt in my mind once I started recovering that I'd come back. I really didn't think my luck had gone bad. I didn't think of my injuries in those terms. I figured I'd gone 17 or 18 years, and I'd been lucky. So it happened two times in a row, but then I was fortunate it hadn't happened before. I also was lucky I was able to survive both injuries and return.

My second comeback wasn't as traumatic as the first one. I wasn't out of action that long, and I was a lot fitter and could handle it better physically. I went to Chicago and began exercising horses—six, seven every morning. My timing hadn't suffered that much, and I was pretty fit and ready. "Might as well start riding again," and I did. My first day back wasn't as dramatic as it was after the 13-month lay-up. I didn't win three that day. But I didn't need it because I felt really good.

Left: During a working vacation in 1969 in Argentina, "The Shoe" gives Latin racing fans a demonstration of his skills in piloting Hay Porque to victory in a race at San Isidro, near Buenos Aires.—*California Thoroughbred Breeders' Association*

Right top: Rounding the turn on Strong, Shoemaker, in the foreground at right, tries for his 7,000th win, at Santa Anita. Arthurian, in back of Strong, won the race, beating Strong by a nose. "The Shoe" chalked up his 7,000th victory the next day, March 14, 1976, on Royal Derby II.—*Michael Gill*

Right bottom: Shoemaker, aboard Royal Derby II in search of his 7,000th win, is out of the picture as Ocala Boy (8), ridden by Steve Valdez, is hotly pursued while setting the early pace. Royal Derby II finished first, "The Shoe" achieving his milestone victory; Ocala Boy crossed the wire 12th and last. —*Michael Gill*

Below: Prior to the 1969 running of the Gran Premio Carlos Pellegrini, Argentina's greatest race, Shoemaker posed for a group portrait with other jockeys competing in the classic at San Isidro, near Buenos Aires.—*California Thoroughbred Breeders' Association*

Overleaf following: "The Shoe" winning his fifth Belmont Stakes, in 1975. Top left: Shoemaker has Avatar (6) away from the gate *(Author's Collection)*. Bottom left: Avatar withstands the bold challenge of Kentucky Derby winner Foolish Pleasure, ridden by Jacinto Vasquez *(Author's Collection)*. Top right: Whipping left-handed, Shoemaker calls on Avatar in the stretch *(Sports Illustrated)*. Bottom right and left: After his victory, Shoemaker takes Avatar to the winner's circle for the traditional ceremony *(Author's Collection)*.

Page 124, top: Aboard Argentine-bred mare Dulcia, Shoemaker wins the $350,000 National Thoroughbred Championship at Santa Anita in 1975. Royal Glint, with Jorge Tejeira riding, was second.—*Allen W. Hopkins*

Page 124, bottom: Wreathed in flowers, Shoemaker is joined in the Santa Anita winner's circle by actor John Wayne and owners Mr. and Mrs. A. W. Stollery after capturing the National Thoroughbred Championship astride Dulcia.—*Allen W. Hopkins*

Dead Aim
on 6,033

WHEN I CAME BACK in 1969 after my second accident, I rode in Chicago and at Bay Meadows, Santa Anita, and Hollywood before the Del Mar meet opened in July, 1970. I won a lot of stakes races during that time—six of them on Fiddle Isle—and three were hundred-granders, so I felt I was back in stride.

It was a kick returning to Del Mar. When I was still an apprentice, in 1949, Del Mar was the first meeting I led. To come back after all these years and be leading rider again was nice. I don't really worry about that kind of thing too much anymore. When I broke my leg, it also broke my string of 17 straight years of being leading rider at Santa Anita and 15 consecutive years at Hollywood Park. But it didn't concern me that much because of the long lay-up time I had recovering from the broken leg. That placed a different perspective on it. If somebody had beaten me while I was riding steadily, I probably would have felt differently.

It was during this Del Mar meeting, in 1970, that I took dead aim on John Longden's record for career winners. I never anticipated being able to break that kind of record early in my career, so I'd never set it up as a goal. But as I got closer to it and knew I could do it, I really wanted it. I rode my 6,000th winner August 8 on a horse named Shining Count, and then the countdown began. As I got nearer the record, which was 6,032 winners, the drama and the tension built up. With all the newspaper guys and TV people following you around, there's always some tension involved. You handle it the best way you can. It took a few days, and then it came down to the last couple of winners. I equaled the record on Esquimal in the ninth race on Saturday, September 5. In one of the early races on Labor Day, September 7, I was on Dares J, a filly trained by Ron McAnally, and I knew she had a real good shot at winning. She broke sharp, and I sent her right to the lead. I let her roll on the turn, and she opened up a pretty long lead. She got a little late in the stretch, but she was too far in front to catch—and that was it. I naturally was happy and relieved it was over. John Longden was there in the winner's circle waiting for me to come back, and he was one of the first to congratulate me. I felt a little bad breaking John's record. I'm sure it meant a lot to him. But records are there to be bettered, so I enjoyed doing it for that reason.

John rode for 40 years, and I broke his record in my 22d year of riding. But when you analyze the conditions we rode under, it's not fair to compare the length of time it took each of us to set our records. Our careers were in different eras really. He rode at a lot of little tracks where they had a few races one day and maybe four or five the next, whereas I could ride eight or nine races a day. He just didn't have that chance for much of his career.

The next year, 1971, was the best of my career as far as winning stakes races. I won 46 to break the record of 43 set by Bill Hartack in 1957. Charlie Whittingham and I teamed up for 29 of those stakes wins with horses he trained, like Ack Ack, who was Horse of the Year, and Turkish Trousers, the champion three-year-old filly of that season. Cougar II was another one. During 1972, I also surpassed Eddie Arcaro's record of 554 career stakes victories, winding up the year with 577. But you know, records really have never meant a helluva lot to me. Sure, when you get close to one, it's nice to go on and break it. I've never set any records as a goal—they just happened. When they come, they come. Records are made and records are broken all the time. All of them will be, eventually, including all of mine.

Charlie Whittingham has been good to me over a period of years, and we've enjoyed tremendous success together. We have the same philosophy about horses—how they should run, how I should ride them, and how he trains them. It all fits together, and that's

Dead Aim on 6,033   127

The photo-finish camera couldn't separate Quicken Tree (3), ridden by Fernando Alvarez, and Fiddle Isle (1), with Shoemaker up, and it was a dead heat for victory in the 1970 San Juan Capistrano Handicap at Santa Anita.—*Santa Anita Photochart*

undoubtedly why we've been successful together. He's had trouble with different owners at times, who've come to him and said, "I don't want Shoe, I want someone else to ride my horse." And he's come to me and said, "This owner wants to do this, and there's not a helluva lot I can do about it." I'd tell him, "Charlie, don't put yourself in the middle. Don't make it tough on yourself. I'll ride another horse. We'll work it out that way." And it's always worked out. The way I feel is if an owner doesn't want me, then I don't want to ride his horse in the first place. Let him put somebody else on, because if I ride his horse and get beat, then it's my fault. I wouldn't want to put that kind of heat on Charlie, to have him say, "Now look, Shoe's my rider and I'm going to ride him. If you don't like it . . . ." I've never wanted it that way.

It happened in 1973 that Mary Jones, who owned Cougar II, wanted to change riders in the Hollywood Gold Cup. I'd been riding Cougar and I'd won several stakes on him, but she wanted Laffit Pincay, which was her privilege. The situation didn't really bother me that much. She felt Laffit would ride Cougar better, so that was that. Laffit's a great jockey, and I was sure he could ride him as well or better than I could. "Fine, I'll ride whatever else you have in the race or pick up another mount," I told Charlie. So I picked up Kennedy Road, a horse Charlie trained for Mrs. A. W. Stollery of Canada. I wanted to win the Gold Cup, but going in I thought Quack, with Don Pierce riding, would win because I thought he probably was the best horse.

Kennedy Road had ability, but he was temperamental. He ran poorly in one race I was on him. He got down in the gate and was kicking in the dirt before the start. Then he came back and ran on the grass and ran pretty well. Right after that, he trained like hell and blossomed out. I just happened to catch him at the right time, because he came up to the Gold Cup really at the top of his game.

Quack made a helluva move at Kennedy Road and actually got about a nose in front, and then he hung. Kennedy Road ran the greatest race of his life, and we won the Gold Cup. Cougar was third. So you see, fate has a lot to do with it. I've always tried to take things in stride, because I learned a long time ago that whatever happens is going to happen for the best. Under the right circumstances, I would have been on Cougar and somebody else would have ridden Kennedy Road. And with a good ride, Kennedy Road would have won the race anyway.

Left top: Displaced as the rider of Cougar II (running third on rail) in the 1973 Hollywood Gold Cup, Shoemaker, on Kennedy Road (inside), narrowly leads Quack, ridden by Don Pierce, in the stretch.

Left bottom: In a prolonged head-and-head duel, Kennedy Road and Quack (4) battle it out down the stretch.

Right top: Running the greatest race of his life under Shoemaker's guidance, Kennedy Road tenaciously withstands Quack's surge to win.

Right bottom: Jubilant in victory, Shoemaker waves to the crowd from atop the flower-draped Kennedy Road.—*Photo sequence by Bill Mochon*

I hit a bit of a slump a few years ago, and I thought seriously then about quitting. Naturally, you have to consider these things when you reach a certain stage in your career. Things weren't going too well, and a lot of people were talking about it. They were taking me off horses and doing this and that and the other. It's true, I was not in great shape. I told myself, "Either you're going to quit or you're going on. You've got a little potbelly and you're not in that good a shape and you're really not riding that well. You've either got to make up your mind you're going to get in real good condition and give it a good shot or hang it up. It's got to be one way or the other—you can't be in the middle." I didn't want to quit that way, and I decided I was going to try. "I'm going to stick in there. I've been lucky all of my life. I'll just keep on punching, and things will get better." I just had the feeling they would.

Above: Shoemaker's 6,000th win, astride Shining Count in the ninth race at Del Mar August 8, 1970, was just another stop along the way to his major objective, John Longden's record of 6,032 career victories.—*William Scherlis*

Left: Riding Thoroughbreds isn't all gold and glory, even for Willie Shoemaker, who is caked with mud after a race.—*Herb Shoebridge*

Above: Joining the world's winningest rider on "Willie Shoemaker Day" at Bay Meadows in 1970 were two veteran riders—Mel Lewis, left, and Merlin Volzke—who were in the lineup when Shoemaker won his first race, in 1949 on Shafter V.—*Author's Collection*

Right: The official photo-finish camera shows the margin of Dares J's victory in giving Shoemaker his 6,033d win to break John Longden's record on September 7, 1970.—*Del Mar Photochart*

And it changed around all of a sudden. I got on a right diet and took care of myself better and trimmed down and lost about five pounds. The weight didn't mean anything, except to my physical makeup. Then I went through a complete physical, with the stress test and all, and I knew then that I was on the right track. When I took the tests, the doctors told me what good shape I was in for a guy my age and that I could compete with guys 25 years old. That helped me mentally, and believe me it prolonged my career. I was beginning to think, "Hell, I can't go any further. I'm old, and I can't do this and I can't do that." Then the doctor tells me, "You're in better condition than most of these 20-year-old athletes." I thought, "Hell, maybe I'm putting myself down too much. I'm on the right track now." And it worked.

Whether it's luck or because I'm determined or whatever, the combination has worked for me most of my life. And I think it'll always work for me. In that period of time, I was lax and I had to shake myself and talk to myself. Of course, heredity has a lot to do with it too, and I come from a family of people who live to ripe old ages. That also helps you mentally when

you get to the age where you begin to think you're getting too old for the riding profession. A guy would say, "He's too old. He shouldn't be riding." And you're thinking, "Maybe they're right, maybe I should say the hell with it and quit." Then you go through these tests, running on a treadmill and all that—the tests are really demanding physically—and the doctor perks you up, making you feel, "I'm not old, I'm going to go on."

Look at John Longden. He rode until he was 59, but he took good care of himself. As long as I feel good and can check myself out in this physical exam every year and the doctors tell me I'm really fit and as long as I think I can ride good, I'm going to continue. I know I'm not as good as I was when I was 25 or 30 years old, but I've got a good head and I know I can analyze a race shaping up better than most jocks because I've been through it more.

Actually, I probably get more charge now out of winning an important race, because, when you get older, they don't come as often as they did in your prime. When I won 485 races that one year, I was winning three and four every day. You tend to become blasé about winning, and you lose track. Then when you're off, like I was for 13 months, you come back and you're not the top dog and you're not winning so many races. Every win has more mean-

Left: Shoemaker signs autographs for his admirers after recording the 6,033d winner of his career on Dares J at Del Mar.—*Sheedy & Long/Sports Illustrated*

Above: Shoemaker accepts the congratulations of John Longden after receiving the 1970 Southern California Athlete of the Year Award at Santa Anita. —*Pasadena Star-News*

The SHOE

ing than it did before, and if it's an important stakes race, then the thrill is just double. Still, for an older guy I did pretty well in '74 and even better in '75, when my mounts earned a total of more than $3.5 million—tops for me in one year. Twelve of my stakes winners were hundred-granders in '74–'75, including the Belmont.

I got more kick out of winning the Belmont Stakes on Avatar in 1975 than I did winning the race on any other horse, except maybe Gallant Man because of the circumstances involved after the 1957 Derby. Avatar, who was owned by Arthur Seeligson from San Antonio and trained by Tommy Doyle, was a colt from California, and he probably should have won the Kentucky Derby. Diabolo, another California colt, bumped Avatar in the stretch in the Derby and turned him sideways. That probably cost Avatar the Derby. Foolish Pleasure went by both of them and won it, but I think Avatar just was unlucky.

He didn't handle the track too well in the Preakness and we were up the track, but it was a different story in the Belmont. We had a good position all the way, made the lead in the upper stretch, and then held off Foolish Pleasure to win by a neck.

Left: It was his 40th birthday, but "The Shoe," on Grits and Gravy (7), wasn't receiving any gifts from Bill Mahorney and Admiral's Son, nose winners according to the photo finish.—*Del Mar Photochart*

Right: With his 44th stakes victory in 1971, achieved aboard Royal Owl in the Junipero Serra Stakes at Bay Meadows, Shoemaker breaks the record for most stakes wins in a single year set by Bill Hartack in 1957. —*Author's Collection*

Overleaf following: Cougar II and "The Shoe" winning the 1973 Sunset Handicap, a hundred-grander. Top left: Shoemaker gets a leg up from trainer Charlie Whittingham on Cougar II in the saddling paddock at Hollywood Park. Bottom left: An equine "character," Cougar II (IA) pauses in the post parade to do a bit of people-watching. Top right: "The Shoe" and Cougar II enter the starting gate. Bottom right: They're off! And it's a good start for Shoemaker and Cougar II. (Sequence continued on page 142)

The running of the 1973 Sunset Handicap continues. Below: Shoemaker restrains Cougar II, saving him for the stretch. Right: Unleashing the burst of speed which made him one of the most popular horses of recent times in the West, Cougar II comes on to win, defeating Life Cycle, with Laffit Pincay up, by a length.—*Photo sequence by Bill Mochon*

Dead Aim on 6,033   143

That was a good win, because I don't get that many shots in the classic races anymore. When I ride in one of those races, it has to be a horse from California because I don't ride in the East and just don't have those connections. I've been away too long. New riders have come up, good riders, and they're there and they're getting those mounts. Any time I get the opportunity now to ride a contender in one of the classics, it's a thrill to me.

On March 14, 1976, at Santa Anita, I passed another milestone, when I got my 7,000th winner. It wasn't anywhere near as exciting for me as breaking Longden's career record back in 1970, but just like that time there was a lot of press coverage and the crowds kept getting bigger as I came close. The funny thing is, the horse I was on, Royal Derby II, hadn't won a race in almost three years.

People keep telling me the 7,000 wins will never be beat. But as I said before, records are broken all the time. For instance, when I won 485 races in 1953, they said there's no way anyone will ever win more races than that in one year. How can it happen? But with more racing and jocks riding more races, it happened. In 1973, Sandy Hawley won 515 races, and then in 1974 Chris McCarron, a bug rider, came along and won 546. He rode almost 2,200 horses during the year. And the same thing is going to happen with winning 7,000 races. Some kid is going to come on the scene and ride 20 years and win 7,000 or 8,000 races. He's going to have to be able to go through a long period of time without injuries and ride many winners for many years. He'll have to have the right temperament, be the right size, everything will have to fit right. But it will happen. It happened to me, so why can't it happen again to somebody else? It's going to happen. I guarantee it.

Left top: The inaugural Rocking Chair Derby in 1973 at Del Mar was the occasion for a reunion in the jockeys' room of "The Shoe" and John Longden (right).—*William Scherlis*

Left bottom: "The Shoe" flashes a winning smile and raises his fist in victory after capturing the Belmont Stakes for the fifth time, on Avatar in 1975.—*Wide World*
(For pictures and description of the race, see color pages 122–3 and caption page 120.)

I really don't know what I'll do when the day finally arrives that I retire. I do know I'll stay in racing if I can. It's been my life and it's what I know and it's what I'd like to do. I believe I could train horses because I know the ins and outs of most of it, and I've been through it from the ground up. The foundation is there for me to train. The only problem with training today is you don't have good, experienced, and reliable help around, guys you know can take care of the horse the way you would. Being there all the time to make sure it's done right would be a downer for me, and I don't think I'd like it. Unless I could have top help all the way through the barn—every groom and exercise boy really good—I wouldn't enjoy being a trainer.

There's so much racing now it's difficult to estimate the ideal size for an outfit. Horses nowadays can't last with all the racing we have. You have to give them a rest once in a while. I'd like to have maybe 20 horses at the track and maybe 30 or 40 at a training center getting ready. You could interchange them if a horse got a little tired or maybe wasn't just right. You could turn one out for a while and bring in another to take his place, one who was almost ready to race. If you could do that number, this would be the ideal way to train a stable of Thoroughbreds.

Left: Thoroughbred racing's most enduring combination has been that of agent Harry Silbert and jockey Willie Shoemaker, a successful team since 1949. —*Vic Stein & Associates*

Above: Crystal Water, a California-bred colt, gives Shoemaker his 112th triumph in a $100,000 race when he wins the 1976 Hollywood Derby.—*Tibor Abahazy*

I don't know where all the outstanding horses are today. When you consider all the Thoroughbreds being produced every year, you have to wonder. The good horses were better a few years ago. Like that year, 1957, when Bold Ruler, Gallant Man, Round Table, Gen. Duke, and Iron Liege were three-year-olds. That was a helluva year. For some reason, we don't seem to have that kind of quality anymore. Maybe because of all the racing today and the demand for horses, they are raced too much as two-year-olds and don't develop as they should. I don't know the answer, but something is wrong somewhere. Nowadays the good horses that show potential are syndicated and retired before they really become mature as racehorses, frequently in their three-year-old season. In my opinion, that's too soon, and it's not good for our game.

If this trend toward premature retirement of our stars continues, it's really going to hurt the sport. And, eventually, you're not going to be able to retire horses for millions of dollars, because the fans are going to get tired of seeing the second-best horses and they're not going to come out and participate. And the money won't be there. People turn out to see good horses and good riders on good horses.

Left: "The Shoe" breezes Dahlia, the world's richest mare, in a morning workout over the grass at Santa Anita during the 1976 season.—*Vic Stein & Associates*

Below: Again showing his ability to rise to the occasion in an important race, Shoemaker urges Riot in Paris to victory over Avatar and jockey Darrel Mc-Hargue in the 1976 Del Mar Invitational Handicap. It was "The Shoe's" 114th success in a $100,000 event.—*Vic Stein & Associates*

Shoemaker's Lifetime Record
(Through March 14, 1976)

Year	Mounts	First*		Second	Third	Pct.	Amount Won*	
1949	1,089	219		195	147	.20	$ 458,010	
1950	1,640	388	(1)	266	230	.24	844,040	
1951	1,161	257		197	161	.22	1,329,890	(1)
1952	1,322	315		224	174	.24	1,049,304	
1953	1,683	485	(1)	302	210	.29	1,784,187	(1)
1954	1,251	380	(1)	221	142	.30	1,876,760	(1)
1955	1,149	307		178	138	.27	1,846,884	
1956	1,229	328		187	165	.27	2,113,335	
1957	1,191	295		183	134	.25	2,544,782	
1958	1,133	300	(1)	185	137	.26	2,961,693	(1)
1959	1,285	347	(1)	230	159	.27	2,843,133	(1)
1960	1,227	274		196	158	.22	2,123,961	(1)
1961	1,256	304		186	175	.24	2,690,819	(1)
1962	1,126	311		156	128	.28	2,916,844	(1)
1963	1,203	271		193	137	.23	2,526,925	(1)
1964	1,056	246		147	133	.23	2,649,553	(1)
1965	1,069	247		161	120	.23	2,228,977	
1966	1,037	221		158	107	.21	2,671,198	
1967	1,044	244		146	113	.23	3,052,108	
1968	104	19		14	11	.18	175,950	
1969	454	97		63	58	.21	1,047,949	
1970	952	219		133	106	.23	2,063,194	
1971	881	195		136	104	.22	2,931,590	
1972	869	172		137	111	.20	2,519,384	
1973	639	139		95	73	.22	2,016,874	
1974	922	160		126	108	.17	2,558,862	
1975	957	215		142	124	.22	3,514,213	
1976**	278	46		41	42	.17	715,880	
Totals	29,207	7,001		4,598	3,605	.24	$58,056,299	

* (1) indicates leader for year.
** Through March 14.

Swaps and Assorted Friends

THE QUALITIES a superior Thoroughbred must have include a kind temperament, an economical, smooth stride, an inherent ability, and a generous heart. In addition, all top horses seem to have one thing in common; they're unusually intelligent. Most of the good horses I've ridden in my career have been blessed with most of these qualities.

Now and then I've come across a good horse who was a bit sulky or strongheaded, but not too often. Horses may not be as intelligent as some other animals, but they certainly aren't stupid. And, of course, some are much smarter than others, the same as with humans and with other animals. It's amazing, but the better the caliber of the horse the more intelligence he possesses. As for stride, most outstanding horses cover the ground smoothly. They don't pick up their feet too high when they're running, but kind of glide over the ground. And I'm positive that smooth action and a good way of going·have a great deal to do with soundness and durability.

SWAPS was the first real good horse I rode. I had seen him at Hollywood Park when he was a two-year-old, but he really wasn't that impressive. He ran about five times there, and he won twice, including a small stakes race.

The first time I got on him was in a six-furlong race at Santa Anita—he was still two, getting ready to turn three—right before the first of the year. He just barely won that day. In the stretch, he was getting late and this horse was catching him. I could tell he had some ability, but on the evidence of that race, I certainly didn't know he was going to be the kind of horse he turned out to be.

The next time Swaps ran is when he impressed me, in the San Vicente Stakes going seven-eighths. Calumet Farm had a horse called Trentonian they thought a lot of. Swaps ran around him, and on the turn he opened up three lengths before Trentonian ever knew what happened. He acted like a top champion horse.

I wanted to ride Swaps in the Santa Anita Derby, but I couldn't because I'd already committed myself to ride Blue Ruler, a colt who was trained by Bill Finnegan and who had won the Del Mar Futurity the previous summer. I told Finnegan that if Blue Ruler won the Futurity—which he did—I'd ride him in the Santa Anita Derby. I would rather have ridden Swaps because I liked him better. So they got John Longden to ride Swaps. John opened up three lengths on Swaps early in the race, and Swaps won by a half-length. I was third, pretty well beaten, on Blue Ruler.

Swaps was an easy horse to ride. He had a lot of speed and was always laying one, two, or three. Sometimes you had the problem of slowing him down early in the race to reserve his strength. He was just a big, free-running freak, a great horse.

He had a tough mouth, but he was sort of green when he was young. As he got older, he got over that. In the Kentucky Derby, coming to the quarter pole, Swaps saw the starting gate parked on the outside of the track and propped, and his ears went up. I had to holler at him and hit him to make him go on by it. He was going to go the other way. He'd look and see things and duck away from them.

Swaps had a beautiful disposition, very kind and gentle. I remember the way they used to lead him by the crowd and let people pet him. But when the gate opened, he wanted to run, that was all there was to it.

He was quick out of the gate. One day he stumbled leaving there, at Santa Anita. He was just too anxious. But he recovered right away and was second in no time.

Swaps wanted to run, so you just had to sit there. When you asked him to run, he'd do it right now. He didn't need much stick—he was trying so hard already—so you just kind of flicked him now and then. You knew he was running fast because you could feel the effort. He had a longer stride than most horses but he had it together. He wasn't one of those big, plodding, long-striding horses. He ran like a sprinter—quick and speedy and shifty.

Swaps never did come from too far out of it because he had so much natural speed. But he could if the pace was really fast. I rode him in Chicago, in the Washington Park Handicap, a flat mile out of the chute. Summer Tan was in there with Eddie Arcaro, carrying 115 pounds, and I was on Swaps, who had 130.

Summer Tan was in front, and he ran the first three-quarters in "seven and four." At the quarter pole, I was swinging Swaps off him, 130 pounds and all. Arcaro couldn't believe it. He looked over, saw that big chestnut colt with his mouth wide open, and did a double take. And Swaps went on and beat Summer Tan fairly easily, by two lengths.

The only thing Swaps couldn't handle was turf that was soft. He only ran on soft turf once, and maybe it's unfair to say he couldn't have handled it the second time. But that particular afternoon he couldn't do it and finished way back. He couldn't get his feet under him and was floundering.

Right: Swaps—"The first real good horse I rode."
—*Vic Stein & Associates*

Swaps had a helluva year in 1956, and he was Horse of the Year. He set the world's record of 1:39⅗ for a mile and seventy yards in a stakes in April at Gulfstream Park. Then at Hollywood Park, in the Argonaut Handicap, he ran a mile in 1:33⅕ and two weeks later won the Inglewood Handicap in 1:39 for a mile and one-sixteenth, and both were world's records.

He equaled the world's record of 1:46⅘ for a mile and one-eighth in the American Handicap, won the Hollywood Gold Cup in 1:58⅗, only two-fifths of a second slower than Noor's record for a mile and a quarter, and then won the Sunset Handicap in 2:38⅕ to break the world's record for a mile and five-eighths.

Swaps ran some great races, but the one I really remember is when he carried 130 pounds and beat Summer Tan in Chicago, running the mile in 1:33⅖ to set a track record at Washington Park.

No question about it, Swaps was a great horse. I'd love to have another one like him.

Facing page: Gallant Man—". . . when he was right, there wasn't a horse he couldn't beat."—*Vic Stein & Associates*

Right: Shoemaker nuzzles Gallant Man, aboard whom he won his first Belmont Stakes in 1957.—*Vic Stein & Associates*

GALLANT MAN was the best natural distance horse, a mile and a quarter and up, I ever rode. He wasn't the soundest horse in the world, but on any given day when he was right, there wasn't a horse he couldn't beat.

I rode Gallant Man in the Kentucky Derby and misjudged the finish line. He wasn't entered in the Preakness, but I rode him in the Belmont Stakes. Arcaro was on Bold Ruler, who had won the Preakness, and he was in front when I came to him at the quarter pole with a handful of horse. Just kidding with him, I said, "How're you doing, Dad?" and he gave me a dirty look. Gallant Man went on and won it by eight lengths and set a track and an American record of 2:26⅗ for the mile and one-half.

The next year, I was on Gallant Man running against Bold Ruler in a race at a flat mile, the Metropolitan. A mile was supposed to be Bold Ruler's dish. Gallant Man just ran by him, beating him handily, by two lengths, at his own game. This was one of those days he could have beaten any horse.

Gallant Man was versatile too. You could place him anywhere you wanted. He could run three-quarters of a mile if he had to, and he could run two miles if he had to. That's what made him a great horse.

He wasn't a big horse; in fact, he was sort of smallish, but he had a big heart. He was nice to ride because you could do anything with him. You could get him to running so he had early speed. If you wanted to save him, you could take him back with one finger, and he'd relax and come right back to you. His ability to relax and run within himself is what made him a great distance horse.

Gallant Man ran several outstanding races, but his Belmont Stakes and his beating Bold Ruler going a flat mile are the two that stick out in my mind as probably the finest races he ever ran.

ROUND TABLE ran some dynamite races for me as a four-year-old and also the next year. I don't think he was as good as either Bold Ruler or Gallant Man, but he stayed sound longer and outlasted them, ran more than they did and in different parts of the country, and won more money.

He was a deceptive horse to watch in a race because he had a long stride and ran with his head held lower than most horses. It made him look as if he was just galloping along and not really running hard. His action was a bit better on turf, if it wasn't soft, than on dirt. He was a little smoother.

In the '59 San Marcos Handicap at Santa Anita, going a mile and a quarter on the grass, he was carrying 132 pounds. Going down the backstretch, he was three or four in front and looking around, and all of a sudden he started buckjumping with me. He was so good and felt so good that he could buckjump and still win. And he ran some tremendous races in Chicago later that year, breaking track records in the Arlington Handicap and the Washington Park Handicap.

One of the things that kept him from being a great horse was that he couldn't run on a muddy, deep, or heavy track. After the San Marcos Handicap, he ran in the Washington's Birthday Handicap at Santa Anita on soft turf and got beat about a quarter of a mile. He just couldn't handle soft turf at all.

But he was a tough horse and versatile. They could ship him anywhere, and he stayed sound a long time. He couldn't beat Gallant Man and Bold Ruler, though. He tried them in the Trenton Handicap in 1957, and he was third. After that, he won many races, avoiding the two top horses. He earned a lot of money—he was the all-time money winner through 1958—because he danced a lot of dances. In fact, I won 21 stakes races on Round Table, and ten were hundred-granders.

Right: Shoemaker, on Gas Energy, second from right, vies for the lead on the clubhouse turn in second race at Santa Anita, March 14, 1976. Trying for his 7,000th win, he was nosed out by Delta Junction, ridden by Sandy Hawley, left foreground. Three races later, Shoemaker won his 7,000th, on Royal Derby II.
—Michael Gill

Arcaro rode Round Table in the Woodward Stakes at Belmont in 1958, at 4–5, and he got beat 17 lengths. I won the race on Clem. The reason I didn't ride Round Table was that Travis Kerr, who owned Round Table, wanted me to sign to ride his horse all year long, and I had Gallant Man and couldn't do it. So Kerr took me off in the Woodward and put Eddie on. That shows you how lucky you can get. I got on a horse called Clem and won, and Round Table was up the racetrack because the track came up muddy and he never could run in the mud.

Above: Round Table—". . . a tough horse and versatile."—*Vic Stein & Associates*

Left bottom: Astride Royal Derby II, a New Zealand-bred seven-year-old horse who was winless in almost three years, Shoemaker reaches another milestone, his 7,000th career victory.—*Vic Stein & Associates*

Left top: Shoemaker and Royal Derby II in the Santa Anita winner's circle after registering his 7,000th victory. At the left are Mrs. E. E. Fogelson (Greer Garson) and trainer Charlie Whittingham. The Fogelsons and Whittingham are co-owners of Royal Derby II.—*Michael Gill*

SILKY SULLIVAN got a lot of publicity because of two races he ran as a three-year-old at Santa Anita when I rode him. Going 6½ furlongs early in the year, he was more than 40 lengths out of it but turned it on in the stretch and won. Then in the Santa Anita Derby, he came from almost 30 lengths back to win again, and by three lengths.

He was an impressive-looking chestnut horse—a big beautiful horse with a lot of flair. His good looks and exciting style made him a hero to sportswriters and the racing public. I don't believe any horse up to that time had received the kind of publicity he did. He had a special train to take him to the Kentucky Derby, and he was everybody's favorite to win. Actually, he wasn't a good horse at all, he just beat some mediocre horses when he won those few times in California.

Silky Sullivan was nice to ride, no problem, especially when he could get up and win from that far back. The only trouble with the colt in the Kentucky Derby was that there was no way he could spot a top horse like Tim Tam, who won the race, that many lengths and expect to beat him. Silky's bubble burst after the Derby, when he was 12th in a field of 14. He went on to the Preakness and still had that same charisma going in, but he fizzled out in that race too, finishing eighth to Tim Tam.

OLDEN TIMES was one of my favorites. Even though he won a lot of stakes, I couldn't classify him as a great horse, like Swaps or Gallant Man, but he was a good one. Olden Times was a game horse with a big heart and a lot of determination. He never gave up. I always liked him, and I have a soft spot in my heart for him.

He probably was the best gate horse I ever was on. I don't believe he was beaten out of the gate even once. He was a length in front of the field every time the man opened the gate. And he could run like hell in the mud.

Olden Times was built sort of like a quarter horse or a sprinter, and his best distance probably was a flat mile out of the chute.

Left: Silky Sullivan—"Silky's bubble burst after the Derby."—*Vic Stein & Associates*

Below: Olden Times—". . . the best gate horse I ever was on."—*Vic Stein & Associates*

However, he did win the San Juan Capistrano Handicap at Santa Anita going a mile and three-quarters on the grass in 1962. He popped out of the gate on the lead a couple of lengths and galloped along, and the only reason he won is because once he got in front he could relax. Had another horse been in there running at him he probably would have been beaten going that distance. But he hung on and won. All he did was gallop them to death.

BOWL OF FLOWERS was a good filly, but I didn't ride her more than once because she was Eddie Arcaro's mount. The only time I rode her was in the Gardenia at Garden State Park, and I'll never forget it. I was switching my stick from right to left and I blew it. She was supposed to be a helluva stick mare, and I dropped my stick. I was back almost last at about the five-eighths pole, and I didn't know what to do to get her moving. So I hit her with my open hand in the stretch, and she got up and won. And I had a sore hand. After that she won a lot of important races. She was a good one.

CICADA was a little bitty filly. In fact, she looked like a muskrat. But what a tough little bitch she was. She carried 128, 129 pounds and won going a distance, won on all kinds of tracks, and won all kinds of money. Out of 42 races, she won 23 times, was second in 8, and third in 6. She also held the record for total earnings by a mare. She was champion of her division three straight years—as a two-year-old, as a three-year-old, and then as the best older filly or mare.

I always had a good feeling about riding Cicada because she was so small and could really do it and never gave up. She got knocked around and knocked down and came back fighting all the time—a tough little filly.

CANDY SPOTS was a good horse, not a great one. He probably was the best horse in the '63 Kentucky Derby, and maybe good enough to have won the Triple Crown if everything had worked out right for him. He injured his hind leg in the Florida Derby, which he won, and they really couldn't get him up to the Kentucky Derby right. He had to be rushed to make the race and he worked three-quarters in 1:10 right before the race. He didn't have the proper time to really prepare and came up a little short in the Derby. He was rank the first part of it, and I wasn't able to place him. Then he ran up on a horse's heels, and I had to check him a couple of times. He made a good move at the quarter pole but hung the last part of it.

Even though he wasn't tight enough for the Derby, that race set him up for the Preakness, and he won it easily, beating Chateaugay, the Derby winner. Then he went on and took the Jersey Derby, but by the time he got to the Belmont Stakes he was dried out and looked it. He was skinny, and you could see all his ribs. He was pretty well strung out because he didn't have the proper seasoning to do all he was asked to do early in the year. But Candy Spots was a big, nice horse to ride, and I won a lot of hundred-granders on him.

Right: Swift Ack Ack, regularly ridden by Shoemaker, won seven stakes in 1971, including the Santa Anita Handicap and Hollywood Gold Cup, and was acclaimed Horse of the Year.—*Herb Shoebridge*

I'll always remember **LUCKY DEBONAIR** fondly because I won the Kentucky Derby on him in 1965 after several years of not winning it. He just did hang on and beat Dapper Dan that day, and if he hadn't been a game kind of colt he never would have won. He was a speed horse, always had a good position. When you asked him to run, he gave you his best.

TOM ROLFE was third in Lucky Debonair's Derby and came back to win the Preakness. I started riding him regularly soon after that. He won four big races at Arlington Park in Chicago—the Citation Handicap, the Chicagoan Stakes, the Arlington Classic, and the American Derby. Then he was shipped to France for the Arc de Triomphe and worked well over there. He could run on any track, but he loved those deep tracks. In the Arc, he got excited and nervous, and when he came to the right-hand turn at Longchamp, he wanted to go left. I had to fight him like hell to get him around that right turn, and this took a lot out of him. He was sixth, but it was a tough year because you had to beat Sea Bird II, who won off by himself. It was one of the better fields in the Arc, and had Tom Rolfe run in the race in another year, he might have won it.

163

I only rode **BUCKPASSER** twice, and he won both times. I won the Everglades at Hialeah on him, and I'll never forget his next race in the Flamingo Stakes. We were on the lead by about a length, and then he kind of eased himself and put his ears up. I reached back and hit him, and right away I was sorry I did it because he propped and really pulled up. Abe's Hope ran by Buckpasser, and at the sixteenth pole, he'd opened up two lengths on us. But I got Buckpasser straightened around and running, and he got up and won.

Buckpasser was really a good horse, but he was a temperamental dude. You couldn't hit him too much—he didn't like the stick at all. You just had to hand-ride him. He never won too many races off by himself—he'd always win by a head, a neck, a half-length. He was difficult to ride, but he could really run.

The first time **DAMASCUS** ran I was on him, and he got beat. The horse that beat him paid $80 and never won another race. But then Damascus came on, and I won many big races on him. Frank Whiteley, his trainer, told me he liked him, and I was working the colt in the morning before he ever ran, so I knew quite a bit about him.

Damascus was third to Proud Clarion in the '67 Kentucky Derby, and he didn't have any excuses. We were in good position all the way, but he hung through the stretch. He didn't have his usual punch for some reason.

He won the Preakness and the Belmont impressively, and with any kind of luck he could have been a Triple Crown winner. It just didn't happen right. I thought he was the best three-year-old of 1967, and he proved it by going on after the Belmont to win a half-dozen more stakes races, including big ones like the Aqueduct, the Woodward, and the Jockey Club Gold Cup—more than enough to make him Horse of the Year.

I always liked Damascus. He was a lazy horse, and you had to make him run most of the time. But when you asked him, he was there. For sheer ability, he might have been as good as any horse I ever rode.

Most of **ACK ACK's** big races were in California. He won the Kentucky Derby Trial as a three-year-old, but his owner at the time, Harry Guggenheim, didn't think he was a distance horse so he didn't run him in the Derby. Ack Ack had a lot of ability, was a very fast horse, and he could really run. He wasn't really a true distance horse. Still, he did win the Santa Anita Handicap and the Hollywood Gold Cup, both at a mile and a quarter, and with topweight on him.

Ack Ack was versatile and a good horse, but he always had trouble changing leads. In fact, a couple of times he almost hit the fence in the stretch. I tried to make him shift leads, and he wouldn't and brushed the fence. Later on, maybe he would change leads or maybe he wouldn't. But he never did get real handy at it. Essentially, he was a speed horse, and as he got older he learned to rate his speed along.

COUGAR II was a South American horse, and a difficult one to ride. You had to neck-rein him. Sometimes he wanted to bear in on horses, and you had a hard time trying to stop him from doing it. Sometimes he'd duck in toward the rail fast. He was disqualified in the

Woodward Stakes in New York because he ducked in and bothered the horse who was third, Tinajero. Cougar won by five lengths, but the stewards took his number down. If he ran by the field fast enough, it didn't matter if he ducked in because he'd be clear of them.

Even though Cougar kept you pretty busy trying to stay out of trouble, I enjoyed riding him because he'd lay back and make that big run, and he looked good doing it.

At Santa Anita in 1970 and in several stakes races at Hollywood Park that summer, **FIDDLE ISLE** impressed me as being as good or maybe better on the grass than any other horse I ever rode. In the San Luis Rey Handicap, at Santa Anita, he set a world's record of 2:23 for a mile and a half on turf. He could accelerate so quickly at times you had to be impressed. When he turned it on, when he was right, it was like driving a Cadillac.

Fiddle Isle, with Shoemaker in the saddle, was a brilliant performer on the grass, winning several important stakes at both Santa Anita and Hollywood Park in 1970.—*Vic Stein & Associates*

There were no hard feelings in 1955 after Eddie Arcaro piloted Nashua to victory over Willie Shoemaker and Swaps in their famous match race at Washington Park.—*Louisville Courier-Journal*

166   *The SHOE*

Comrades in Silks

MANY ELEMENTS distinguish the great rider from the average one—balance, intelligence, the ability to switch the whip from one hand to the other and back again, making the right moves most of the time, and a rapport with horses. Most of the outstanding riders have all these qualities.

Being in the right spot at the right time during a race comes with experience. The more a jockey rides the better he becomes at placing his horse. But sometimes it's instinctive. And the guy who has the instinct, the natural feel for position, has it right away except that he improves on it day by day. It's impossible to make all the right moves all the time, but if a rider can do it 80 percent of the time he's way ahead of the game.

Techniques have changed quite a bit since I began riding back in 1949. Many South American riders have come to this country, and they have strongly influenced the general style here. Jockeys ride with much shorter stirrups and sit up a little higher and closer to the horses' necks than they did 20 or 25 years ago. Shorter stirrups raise the legs, making the body more compact, and the rider isn't moving around all over the horse like he used to in the old days. And this minimizes the effect of weight on a horse. The more compact the rider and the less he moves during a race, the better he can help the horse carry the load on his back. Just as they have in every other sport, the techniques of race riding have improved. And so have riders generally.

John Longden, Eddie Arcaro, and a few of their contemporaries could ride in any era because they were outstanding riders. If they were competing today, they would have adopted the current style and would have been just as successful.

As an example of how today's techniques are different, there weren't too many riders when I came around who could switch the stick from right to left or from left to right. Only the top ones could. Longden and Arcaro were two who could do it, of course, and Jack Westrope and Johnny Gilbert, who were also great riders. The rest never even attempted it; these guys had adopted a pattern and stayed with it. They had a different seat and style, and they wanted to get real low on a horse and look pretty. Most jocks riding today don't even think about that.

It's a great edge if you can hit a horse on either side and do it the right way. I made sure I learned how to do it when I started. From the beginning, I practiced all the time. I'd be back in the pack and couldn't get a horse to try by hitting him on the right side, so I'd try switching my stick to my left hand. And it really helped me. Many horses had never been hit on the left side. When I hit them on the left it would surprise them, and they'd take off and run. I won many races for that reason alone.

EDDIE ARCARO was the greatest rider I ever saw. In his prime, he was really terrific. He could do just about anything you can do on a horse, and do it well. And, of course, he was extremely successful. Among his many accomplishments was riding two Triple Crown winners —Whirlaway in 1941 and Citation in 1948.

In addition to his ability, he was an articulate guy and probably was the jock most instrumental in elevating the prestige of riders, especially among Thoroughbred owners and society people. Eddie's intelligence carried over into his riding. He had everything. He looked better on a horse when he was riding than most guys. Everything he did, he did with a flair. He made it look good, and it was good.

I was aware of him and his talent before I saw him in action for the first time. He came to Santa Anita every winter, but it wasn't until 1950 that I got the chance to see Eddie ride in person.

One day during that Santa Anita season I was talking to Al Shelhamer, who is a steward in California now but was then the patrol-film analyst. He pointed out how smoothly Arcaro left the gate—the timing and everything was always just right. Eddie was hand-riding leaving the gate, and you could see how smooth he and the horse were together. That's the first time I'd ever seen anybody with that flair. I don't know whether Eddie had to work at it or whether it was instinctive, but he had it, whatever it was. He could do everything. He was a good gate boy, had the intelligence to make the right moves, and was in a good position when he needed it. And there was nobody like him for finishing on a horse. Eddie always was hard to beat, because he was so good. I know he beat me more times than I beat him.

After I saw him ride a few times, I thought about copying his style, but then I decided that would be a mistake. For one thing, we were built differently—he was taller than I was—and his technique was so different from mine. I felt that if I didn't do my own thing, I might be hurting myself.

Eddie rode with a long stirrup on the left side and a short one on the right, commonly known as acey-deucey. In those days, most of the riders dropped their left stirrup two or three inches or even four or five inches lower than the right. In fact, Jack Westrope looked like he

Eighteen-year-old Willie Shoemaker was a star on the rise in 1950 at Hollywood Park when he sat alongside established veterans (from left) John Gilbert, Jack Westrope, and Johnny Adams.—*Author's Collection*

was riding about a foot lower on the left side. Eddie was sort of a tall guy for a jockey, so when he bent over on a horse he couldn't take a long hold on the reins—he'd have to take more of a medium hold.

Eddie advised me and was good to me. When I went to New York the first time, he recommended me as a good rider to all the right people. He really helped me get started fast because he knew all the owners of the big stables in the East, and they had the top horses.

JACK WESTROPE was one of the best riders of his era and led the nation in winners back in 1933. He was a strong rider and had all the attributes of Arcaro. Possibly, he was a little wilder and more headstrong than Eddie, but he was a great race rider.

Westrope carried the acey-deucey thing to an extreme, and I believe the reason he did was that he broke his left leg once and couldn't really bend it that much when he started in riding again. So he dropped his left iron, and after a while he felt comfortable that way and just went on riding with his left stirrup much longer than the right.

I remember riding in a race at Hollywood Park with Westrope once when I was an apprentice. He liked the horse he was riding so much that he bet on him. I was in front of him on a horse trained by Red McDaniel; then Westrope comes up and he's whipping left-handed. I didn't know who the jock was, but I saw him whipping and I stuck my stick out. Jack hit my stick and lost his, and I beat him by a nose. He was hot, really hot. He was ready to kill me. Looking at the movies, he told the stewards, "Look at that little son of a bitch. Are you gonna let him get away with that?" They said, "He didn't do anything but stick his whip out and you hit it." He lost his money, and that's why he was so hot, but he cooled out later.

I recall another time when Westrope came up to me in the stretch and locked his left leg around my right leg. I was really young at the time. When we got near the finish, he must have thought better about it because he turned me loose. I guess he realized the stewards would see it, when they looked at the movies of the race. I beat him, but I wouldn't have if he hadn't turned me loose from that leg-lock. But leg-locking is in the past. No one does it anymore. With the shorter stirrups used today, riders' legs are too high, so it can't be done. But even if it could be done, you couldn't get away with it, because it would show up in the patrol films.

Riders like Westrope and Arcaro began their careers before there were patrol films, and just about anything went. Race riding then was a lot rougher and more dangerous than it is now. You had to know all the tricks and protect yourself because if you didn't you had no chance to last.

JOHNNY ADAMS was short, but he was stocky and unusually strong. He never hit a horse much; he just hand-rode them, and he really got a lot of run out of a horse. He was tough to beat from the eighth pole home. He never over-rode. He kept that long hold all the way through the lane and you'd think, "I've got him now." You'd swear you had him all the time, but you never got him.

Adams was leading rider for winners three times in his career, and he rode many great grass horses. He rode the grass course at Arlington Park probably better than anyone I've ever known. He really handled the course super. He could go to the front if he had to, but he also could come from behind, save ground, and make his move. He did the right thing at the right time 90 percent of the time.

JOHN LONGDEN was the greatest competitor I ever rode with. He'd try to beat you any way he could, and he usually did. He probably taught me more about riding—just by watching the things he did in our races together—than any other jockey I ever rode with.

We had a lot of ups and downs in our relationship during my career. In the beginning, when I was very young, I'd get mad at him because of the things he did to me in a race, like shut me off coming out of the gate. And he did them all the time. But that was what he was supposed to do as a rider and to win races, and later on, I learned to appreciate his technique.

A lot of the tricks that were effective for John when he was riding are used very little now. One of the things he did was put his horse on the lead and then weave in and out. Today it would be difficult for him to do that. But it was all right in the old days, because you could get away with it. And if John could get away with anything, it was part of the game.

If he was on a horse with speed, he'd pop out of the gate and get to the front if he could, and then dare you to try and get by him. Once he was on the lead, the racetrack usually was his. He had positions on the track where he could move out into you, then move back in, and leave you out there. The movies really wouldn't show it that well. He knew just the places where he could do these things and get away with them most of the time.

A young jock in a race might be on a horse with speed, and John would go to him and say something like, "Look, kid, let's don't kill each other off. I'm on the inside, so you just take back and let me go on and we can go from there. Right?" When the kid did that, more times than not the race was over, because John could get the position he liked—and that was it, all the way to the finish.

John liked to talk to the other riders in the middle of a race, especially the younger ones. He'd say, "Watch out what you're doing," to get them out of position or to get into a position he wanted. These are some of the things that made him such a great rider and why

Young Willie Shoemaker, fresh from the ranks of the apprentice jockeys in 1950, listens intently to John Longden's words at Hollywood Park.—*Vic Stein & Associates*

he did so well. He was really good at his trade. He had a different way of doing it than guys like Arcaro and Westrope. But his way was very effective.

He rode with his stirrups a little shorter on both sides than most riders and sat kind of up on a horse's neck. He was a short guy, anyway. He'd get right up on a horse's neck, chirp to him, pump him—anything to make a horse run. And he set a trend. You can go back and look at all the distance races that were run, and if John was in the race, you can bet the pace was a lot faster than it would be today. He made his horses last on the lead. Going a mile and a sixteenth, he'd send one out of the gate and set a fast pace, and somewhere along the way he'd give the horse a breather. Then he'd cut him loose again and make him last the distance and win. He had a knack for doing that. He'd be three in front at the half-mile, and maybe you'd start moving up and could get within a length or so of him after you went a little farther. But while you were moving up, he'd be giving his horse a breather. When you got to him then, he'd pick up his horse and hit him about three times and open three more lengths on you. That'd kill your horse and you too, and all you could say was, "Aw, hell, it's all over."

No doubt about it, Longden was a master. He got me a jillion times and beat me with all his tricks. I didn't appreciate a lot of it in the beginning, but eventually I learned those tricks and used them when I could.

John, of course, had a tremendous career. He rode for 40 years and won a ton of races, including the Triple Crown in 1943 with Count Fleet. He ended his career at age 59 the way every race rider hopes he can, with a winner, on George Royal in the 1966 San Juan Capistrano at Santa Anita. He became a trainer, and he's been a success at that too. It was a big thrill for me to ride his first winner as a trainer. One of the horses he developed was Majestic Prince, who won the Kentucky Derby and the Preakness in 1969.

I have great admiration for John. I respect the things he could do and that he could do them so well. He and I are good friends, and I like him very much.

Another outstanding jockey who rode in the same era as Westrope, Arcaro, and Longden was **RALPH NEVES.** He was a rider for 31 years, and he's among the top ten all-time winners.

Technique-wise, he rode with longer stirrups than most of the jockeys in those days. He would lean over to the left side a little when he was riding, and a lot of his horses wanted to lug in to the rail. He was a good whip-rider. He probably didn't hand-ride as well as someone like Arcaro. He had a good head on him, and he knew what he was doing.

Ralph was kind of a tough guy to ride with because he wouldn't give you much of a shot. He'd shut you off even if you were out of contention. If you were next-to-last or even last, he'd still shut you off, just for practice. But he was a good guy and I liked him. Once you

Left: In the jockeys' room at Hollywood Park in 1962, Eddie Arcaro, who had retired in 1961, takes some friendly needling about his weight from Johnny Longden and Shoemaker for the benefit of the cameraman.—*Vic Stein & Associates*

knew him and what to expect of him, he was fun to ride with. You just had to ride your race accordingly.

I remember he shut me off about three times in a row, and I was getting a little tired of it. I said to myself, "Okay, Ralphie, it'll happen one of these days." And it did. We were up at Tanforan and he was on the inside, in post position two or three and I was in five or six. Going to the first turn, two horses were outrunning us. He was right in behind them, and I had him outrun to the outside. He was having trouble holding his horse, and he wanted me to let him out. I said, "Oh no. You get out the same way you got in." He was all over heels, pulling up and snatching, but he made it all right. I guess I really shouldn't have done it. I thought I'd teach him a lesson, and from that time we got along real well. He never bothered me, and I never bothered him.

STEVE BROOKS was a strong guy. He'd ride any kind of horse in any place, he didn't care where. Anything with hair on it, bring him out and Steve would ride him. And he did a great job of it. He really was a whip-rider. He could hit a horse before he ever got out of the gate. First jump, when the gates opened, he'd hit him. He was a good rider, and he used his head. His strong point probably was the whip. He had a helluva career too, winning almost 4,500 races. Among these were many big stakes races on some outstanding horses, including the Kentucky Derby on Ponder in 1949.

TED ATKINSON was called "The Slasher" because of the way he used the whip. He'd hit a horse on the upswing and then again on the downswing, and it was effective for him. He was a hard jock to beat too. You thought he was riding his horse all out—the reins might be loose and dangling—but he'd keep him running, and sometimes you couldn't get by him. Atkinson won about 3,800 races, putting him among the leaders in total career wins. He was the regular rider of Tom Fool, who was Horse of the Year in 1953, and he won the Preakness and the Belmont Stakes in 1949 on Capot.

BILL HARTACK has a very unorthodox riding style. I don't believe I've ever seen another jock with one quite like it. He moves around a lot on a horse. He sort of twists his body and bounces up and down. That's the way he's looked to me. But it sure has worked for him because he got the job done. He's won a ton of races in his life and a lot of big ones, including the Kentucky Derby five times—and that's something only he and Eddie Arcaro have done. At his peak, horses ran well for him, and he had a good head on him. He knew where he was at all times.

Right: A bronze bust of Shoemaker stands in the paddock area at Santa Anita. Joining the champion rider at the April, 1971, unveiling were (from left) Harry Silbert, John Longden, and Shoemaker's wife, Babbs.—*Author's Collection*

MANUEL YCAZA was a good rider, no question about it. He had good style, could hand-ride, whip, and do anything anyone else could do on a horse. But he had a fiery temperament, and he got into a lot of trouble because of it. He'd take advantage, overdo it, and get set down. He won the 1964 Belmont Stakes on Quadrangle and some other big races, but he should have had a better career than he had. And he would have if he'd used his head more than he did. Still, Manuel was a likable guy. But he was a taker, not a giver. When he was riding, he'd rarely give the other guy a break. He was always taking advantage—shutting everybody off and that kind of thing. The guy who does that all the time is going to get it himself once in a while.

In my opinion, a fiery temperament like Ycaza's can be a disadvantage. My grandfather told me a long time ago, "When you lose your head, your ass goes with it." And I haven't forgotten it.

BRAULIO BAEZA is one of the greatest riders in racing today. He has the kind of temperament I'm partial to. I like the controlled way he sits on a horse. He'll wait and make his move when he thinks it's right, and it usually is right. He's a cool cat, and I like that.

He can hand-ride well, whip with either hand, and has the qualities a good rider must have. But his biggest plus is his coolness, how he sizes up a race and reacts to a particular situation. He never gets panicky. He's tall and slim and reminds me of Arcaro when I see him walking away. They have the same look.

Braulio was leading money-winning rider in the country four straight years and has won many big stakes races on some top horses. He won the Kentucky Derby on Chateaugay in 1963 when I was third on Candy Spots. Then after I won the Preakness on Candy Spots, he came back on Chateaugay and beat us again in the Belmont Stakes. When he won the Belmont in '61, he was on a long shot—Sherluck, at 65–1.

ISMAEL (MILO) VALENZUELA was a good rider when he was young, and he won some great races, like the Kentucky Derby in 1958 on Tim Tam and many stakes races when he was Kelso's regular rider. He won the Preakness twice too. He was strong, could whip with either hand, and had most of the attributes of a good rider.

I don't think he used his head very much off the racetrack, and it got him into trouble. I think his problem was he liked to play around with the girls and drink, that sort of thing. I'm not knocking him, but I think he overdid it and did it at the wrong times, and it was bound to hurt his career. You've got to be in top condition when you ride every day, and that stuff knocks you right on your ass. And when you get a little older, it becomes even more difficult.

Left top: Shoemaker is joined at Del Mar by five fellow Hall-of-Fame members. From left: Johnny Adams, Eddie Arcaro, Ralph Neves, "The Shoe," John Longden, and Laffit Pincay.—*George Andrus*

Left bottom: America's greatest riders today. From left, top row: Jorge Tejeira, Jorge Velasquez, Fernando Toro, Braulio Baeza, Angel Cordero, Darrel McHargue. Bottom row: Donald Pierce, Sandy Hawley, Shoemaker, and Laffit Pincay.—*Tibor Abahazy*

As I look back on it, I think Milo probably tried to imitate Eddie Arcaro. He tried to pattern his style after Eddie's, with the hand-riding and the way Eddie used to get down and push one without his fanny bouncing up and down. He'd just be right with that horse. All the riders in those days tried to copy Eddie because his style was the best.

The first time I saw **SANDY HAWLEY** in a race, I didn't think he was a top rider. Turning for home, he put the stick in his mouth to switch it to the other hand, and I said to myself, "A good rider doesn't do that—that's for a beginner." But the more you're around him, the more you realize he is a top rider. He has the ability to make the move at the right time, and he gets a lot of run out of horses.

He's a bit unorthodox looking on a horse, but he does too many right things not to be considered a top rider. He's stronger than he looks, even though he's light. As long as Sandy remains healthy, I don't see why he can't do just about anything he wants to do in racing. He has a great temperament. If he gets in trouble and gets beat, he doesn't flip his lid and worry about it for two or three races and screw up another race because he's worried about the race that just went by.

Hawley is busy on a horse, but his style is not as radical as Hartack's. He looks better than Hartack—he has a better seat. He's an aggressive sort of kid, hitting horses on the shoulder, hollering at them, whistling at them, and doing all sorts of things to make them run. And it works for him. Sandy was the first one to break my record of 485 winners in a single year, when he rode 515 winners in 1973. Sandy rides in this country a lot now, but he's from Canada. He's won Canada's biggest race—the Queen's Plate—a number of times, once on Kennedy Road, a Canadian colt.

LAFFIT PINCAY is one of the great riders of all time. He has all the attributes of a great one. He's strong, has a good head, and he's a terrific finisher. He has exceptional strength, and I don't think there's anyone around today that can finish on a horse any better than he can.

Left: After riding with Laffit Pincay, in 1966, Shoemaker tabbed the Panamanian as a potential champion, a prediction which has come true.—*Tibor Abahazy*

Right: Flanked by his contemporaries, Shoemaker holds a trophy almost as tall as himself after a special all-star jockeys' race in 1961 at Turf Paradise, in Phoenix, Arizona. Holding trophies (from left), the jockeys are Pepper Porter, Eddie Burns, Donald Pierce, Peter Moreno, John Longden, Eddie Arcaro, Shoemaker, Henry Moreno, Bill Harmatz, and Alex Maese.—*Author's Collection*

Eddie Arcaro was an aggressive, powerful rider and that's the way Laffit is. He makes horses run; he makes them do things. With all his power, Laffit has style. He hand-rides beautifully, and he does everything on a horse with polish.

I saw Pincay ride for the first time in 1966 in Chicago, and he impressed me then. He was young and strong and sat cool and hand-rode well. I could see he had a lot of potential and, if nothing happened to him, he was going to make it. And, of course, he has, in a big way.

He was the nation's leading rider for money won five straight years, 1970 through 1974, and he was the first jock whose mounts earned more than $4 million in a single year, in 1973.

ALVARO PINEDA was coming into his own when he was killed in a freak accident in the starting gate in 1975 at Santa Anita. It's just too bad that it happened when it did, because he was just beginning to settle down. He used to be a wild guy. Alvaro was a family man, didn't drink anymore, and had straightened out his whole life. He was a top rider and looked good on a horse. His style was right, and he was a good hand-rider. He could do it all.

ANGEL CORDERO is another top rider. He's a happy-go-lucky guy, and he sort of rides that way, with a lot of gusto. He's always smiling and happy, and he has that same attitude when he's racing. And horses sure run for him. He won the Kentucky Derby on Cannonade in 1974 and both the Derby and the Belmont in 1976 on Bold Forbes.

I saw **DARREL McHARGUE** ride for the first time in 1974 when he came to Hollywood Park and won the Hollywood Lassie Stakes on Hot 'n Nasty. I'd heard he was a pretty good rider from the East, and he looked it. Then he came to Del Mar the following summer and wound up leading the standings.

He's young, fairly light, and has all the technique of a good rider. For a young guy, he's cool and seems to know what race riding is all about. He's good with the whip. He can hit right-handed and left-handed and knows when to hit a horse and when not to hit one and not to overdo it. He hand-rides well and looks good. As far as I can see, Darrel has everything it takes to be a top rider right now.

DON PIERCE is one of the best. I think he's underrated, and he doesn't get the chance he deserves considering the caliber of rider he is. The proof is that when he does get the opportunity in a big race, he's always right there on the money. Yet, he's never received proper recognition.

Don is intelligent and does everything a good rider can do, and he does it well. He rides hard and he can really finish.

The French rider **YVES SAINT-MARTIN** doesn't sit a horse like jockeys do in this country because in Europe the style is a lot different than ours. Still, his technique looks more Americanized than I'd expected after all the European riders I've seen. He has a great mind and knows where he is on the track, and he can adapt his riding style for different countries. Saint-Martin won nine French championships by the time he was 30 years old, so you know he's a good one.

LESTER PIGGOTT, an English rider, probably is even more adaptable than Saint-Martin because he has raced in more countries. He's competed on all kinds of courses and on all kinds of horses and been successful doing it. He's probably the top jockey in England today. Piggott has won more of England's classic races than any other rider in the modern era, and he's been national champion many times.

Riders in Europe think we look bad, and we think they look bad, because of the contrast in styles. But there are really only a few differences between their riding techniques and ours. The basic elements of the sport are the same all over; otherwise jockeys couldn't compete with riders in other countries. It's in the way these basics are performed that makes the styles a little different.

If you really get down to the technical part of race riding, the top jocks all look about the same in certain vital areas. It's just like other sports—take golf, for example. A golfer's grip or stance may be different from another's, but when golfers hit the ball they look almost the same. And you can see that similarity in the styles of your outstanding riders.

A Day in the Life...

WHEN I HAVE TO GO to the racetrack to work a horse in the morning, I'll usually get up at about six o'clock. On other days, I'll sleep till around eight or eight-thirty. I like to do a few calisthenics when I first get out of bed. My routine is 50 sit-ups and 50 push-ups. That exercise wakes me up, gets the blood pumping, and makes me feel good starting out the day.

Normally, it's about ten o'clock when I get back home from the track after breezing a horse. And that's when I have my breakfast. It usually consists of whole-wheat toast and Raisin Bran. I like to add fruit, either peaches or bananas, to my cereal. Or I might vary my breakfast by having two scrambled eggs, whole-wheat toast, sliced tomatoes, and a glass of skim milk. I top it off with vitamins, and that's it.

I prefer whole-wheat breads to the processed white breads because I believe they're more nutritious. A few years ago, on the recommendation of Dr. Toby Freedman, an associate of Dr. Robert Kerlan's, I changed my diet to a more natural one and started taking vitamins regularly along with it. I'm sure vitamin E has helped me a lot, because I'm stronger and have more stamina than I had before. Now I can ride eight or nine horses on a card and not feel tired like I used to a couple of years back .

With the new diet, I lost four or five pounds and trimmed down. I never had a weight problem, so losing a few pounds isn't the important thing. It's just that eating right makes me feel better and I'm doing better physically.

After breakfast at home, I drive to the track, have a massage in the jockeys' room to loosen up, and then get into my silks to ride my first race. During the day in the jocks' room, I might drink a cup of coffee, and that's all. Some riders eat lunch, then force it up. I'm lucky

I don't have to worry about my weight, but most of the other guys do, and they have to put in time in the sweatbox to get their weight down to the maximum set for the race. They'll usually lose maybe two or three pounds. You can take off more than that, but this tends to weaken some riders.

Jockeys go through the same routine for every race. Just before each race you weigh out with your saddle. Then you go to the walking ring. Here your horse is brought in from the paddock, where he's been saddled. The trainer helps you mount—gives you a leg up—and you go to the track. Right after the race you weigh in with your saddle again—the race result isn't official until you do. When you get back to the jockeys' room, you get out of your silks. You change them for every race unless you happen to be riding for the same owner in the next one.

If you have a mount in every race on a card—you don't always, of course—there isn't time in between to do much of anything. The jocks play cards a lot, and that's what I do mostly. Sometimes I play table tennis or I might watch TV.

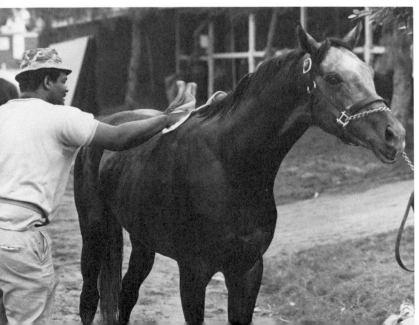

Left top: A typical day in the life of Willie Shoemaker may begin with him arriving at the racetrack early to drill personally a Thoroughbred he might be riding in an important stakes race at some future date. In this instance, "The Shoe" is on the scene to breeze the two-year-old colt Duke Wayne for trainer Charlie Whittingham at Hollywood Park.

Left bottom: Every day is "bath night" for the pampered Thoroughbred. After his workout, Duke Wayne is washed off by his groom. The colt will then be covered by a blanket to insure a gradual return to his normal body temperature, walked on the tow ring until "cooled out," and returned to his stall.

Facing page . . .
Left top: After a conference with Shoemaker in the racing secretary's office regarding the day's riding schedule and upcoming engagements, agent Harry Silbert lines up a stakes mount with trainer Roger Clapp (background) while Willie chats with one of his many young fans.

Right top: An early arrival in the jockeys' room, "The Shoe" scans the Daily Racing Form while his breakfast is being prepared. Frequently, however, he drives home for breakfast after working a horse in the morning.

Left bottom: A massage by the jockeys' room masseur, Hans Beck, loosens and tones Willie's muscles as he kibitzes with fellow rider Raul Ramirez.

Right bottom: Whiling away the time before his first mount of the afternoon, "The Shoe" plays a game of cards with masseur Hans Beck and Frank Smothers, who is in charge of racing silks, or "colors," as they are called. Later, between races, he might play table tennis or watch TV.

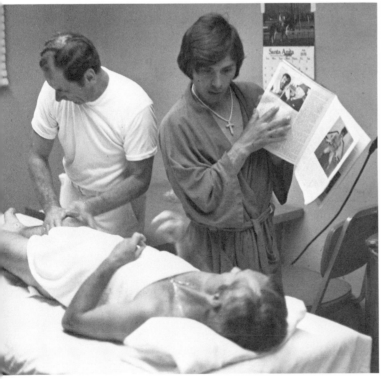
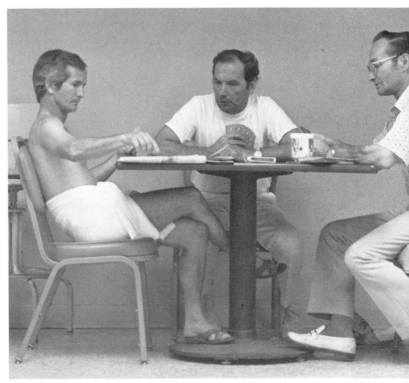

Left top: In Shoemaker's dressing area, Jimmy Hood, Willie's longtime valet, prepares the rider's tack, including boots, helmet, and saddle. Hood and Shoemaker started out together as aspiring jockeys working as exercise boys for Hurst Philpot in 1948. However, Hood's saddle career was curtailed when he grew too large.

Right top: Shoemaker dons silks for his first mount of the afternoon, Ruby E.

Left bottom: Back in the jockeys' room after finishing second on Ruby E., Shoemaker weighs out on the scales for his mount in an upcoming race.

Facing page . . .
Left top: After weighing out, "The Shoe" goes to the paddock, where he receives instructions from veteran trainer M. E. (Buster) Millerick prior to climbing aboard Mark's Place, his mount in the featured Marina del Rey Handicap at Hollywood Park.

Right top: In the saddling paddock, Shoemaker gets a leg up on Mark's Place from trainer Millerick.

Bottom: Accompanied by a stable pony and his rider, Shoemaker parades postward astride Mark's Place, a strong contender in the mile and one-sixteenth event.

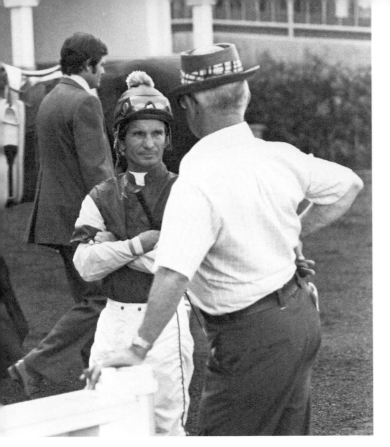

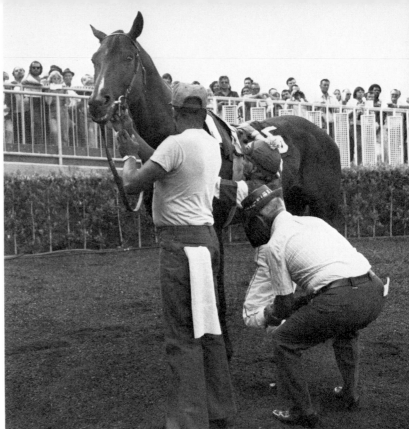

Top: The field of six horses, including Mark's Place (5), breaks from the gate.

Left: The pack is well bunched in the run to the clubhouse turn.

Facing page . . .
Top: With the wire in sight, Mark's Place and Shoemaker are narrowly in front of the hard-charging Pisistrato (4), ridden by Laffit Pincay.

Left bottom: Unable to hold off Pisistrato's bold challenge, Mark's Place and Shoemaker are nosed out at the line.

Right bottom: Beaten by the smallest of margins, "The Shoe" returns Mark's Place to be unsaddled.

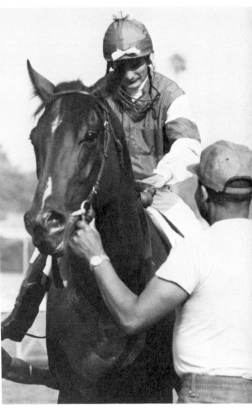

When the races are over, I come home and have dinner, usually around seven-thirty or eight o'clock. I'll eat chicken or fish, a salad, and perhaps a vegetable—peas, green beans, or carrots. I only eat steak maybe once a week, simply because I like fish or chicken better and they contain less cholesterol than steak. My diet doesn't change too much. But I really enjoy the food I eat, so I don't have to force myself to stay on this particular diet.

I only eat two meals a day, unless I have to appear at a sports luncheon or something similar. I might have a small portion there, but even that throws my diet a bit off kilter. Whether I'm riding or not, I usually eat at about the same time and have the same type meals every day.

After dinner, I just relax and watch television or play cards with my wife Babbs or backgammon with some friends. I'll catch the late news on TV and then go to bed about eleven-thirty. I don't have any problems sleeping, and I try to get at least eight hours' rest every night. If I have to get up early to work a horse, then I compensate by going to bed early that night.

On the days I have off during the Del Mar, Santa Anita, and Hollywood Park seasons, I might play tennis or occasionally golf in the daytime. My home isn't too far from Santa Anita and Hollywood Park. When I'm riding at Del Mar, which is just north of San Diego, I rent a house near the track. And sometimes, of course, I fly East for a stakes race, but other than that my days and nights are pretty much the same.

I don't see too many movies, but I do read a book now and then when I have time. I like mystery stories and good nonfiction historical novels. Mostly, even when I'm off, I prefer to stay home in the evening.

Facing page . . .
Left top: His day's work completed, Willie weighs in with Clerk of Scales Dean Scarborough for the final time during the afternoon.

Right top: After showering, Shoemaker changes into the clothes he brought with him in the morning. Here, garment bag in hand, he talks with valet Jimmy Hood and prepares to depart.

Bottom: Leaving the jockeys' room, Shoemaker walks through the tunnel to the area where he parked his car. The working day which began more than 12 hours earlier is about to end as he prepares to get into his car for the drive home. Tomorrow is another day, and there will be nine more races and several opportunities to do what he has done more of than any other rider in the history of horse racing—win. —*Photo sequence on pages 182–8 by Michael Gill*

Right: Shoemaker enjoys a glass of champagne and chats with his mother, Ruby, at the wedding reception after his 1961 marriage to Babbs.—*Author's Collection*

Facing page . . .
Left top: Willing to tackle any sport, Shoemaker tries his skill at bowling.—*Richard Bandurian*

Right top: "The Shoe" takes a healthy cut at the ball during a celebrity baseball game at Dodger Stadium.—*Pasadena Star-News*

Left bottom: A low-handicapper on the links, Shoemaker and champion golfer Lee Trevino await their time to tee off in a taping session for Trevino's golf television program.—*Author's Collection*

Right bottom: Despite the disparity in height, Shoemaker and former Los Angeles Lakers professional basketball star Elgin Baylor are friendly rivals on the tennis court.—*Author's Collection*

Right: Golfing buddies Willie Shoemaker and Frank Sinatra.—*Author's Collection*

Bottom: Shoemaker and wife Babbs stroll on the beach at Del Mar.—*Sheedy & Long/Sports Illustrated*

Stakes Races Won by Shoemaker

	Date	Track*	Stakes Race	Horse	
1.	10–26–49	BM	George Marshall Claiming H.	AL	
2.	7–11–50	Hol	Hollywood Oaks	MRS. FUDDY	
3.	7–29–50	DM	Bing Crosby H.	IMPERIUM	
4.	8–9–50	DM	Oceanside H.	SPECIAL TOUCH	
5.	8–12–50	DM	Coronado H.	WAR POPPY	
6.	9–4–50	DM	Del Mar H.	FRANKLY	
7.	11–11–50	BM	Bay Meadows H.	FRANKLY	
8.	1–20–51	SA	Santa Margarita H.	SPECIAL TOUCH	
9.	2–3–51	SA	Santa Anita Maturity**	GREAT CIRCLE	(1)
10.	2–17–51	SA	San Antonio H.	ALL BLUE	
11.	4–28–51	BM	Bay Meadows H.	MOONRUSH	
12.	5–5–51	BM	Children's Hospital H.	COALTOWN	
13.	5–11–51	Hol	Hollywood Premiere H.	SPECIAL TOUCH	
14.	5–12–51	Hol	Will Rogers H.	GOLD NOTE	
15.	5–19–51	Hol	Golden State Breeders' H.	MOONRUSH	
16.	6–30–51	Hol	Westerner S.	GRANTOR	
17.	7–11–51	Hol	Cinderella S.	THATAWAY	
18.	8–25–51	DM	Del Mar Derby	GRANTOR	
19.	9–22–51	Aqu	Beldame H.	THELMA BERGER	
20.	10–1–51	Bel	Vosburgh H.	WAR KING	
21.	10–16–51	Bel	Champagne S.	ARMAGEDDON	
22.	12–15–51	GGF	Golden Gate H.	PALESTINIAN	
23.	1–26–52	SA	Santa Margarita H.	BED O' ROSES	
24.	2–22–52	SA	Washington's Birthday H.	PET BULLY	
25.	8–9–52	DM	La Jolla H.	ARROZ	
26.	9–27–52	BM	Peter Clark H.	DON REBELDE	
27.	12–13–52	Tan	Tanforan H.	SIMONSEZ	
28.	2–12–53	SA	Lincoln's Birthday H.	STRANGLEHOLD	
29.	2–14–53	SA	San Antonio H.	TRUSTING	
30.	3–14–53	Tan	Bay District H.	ATOMIC SPEED	
31.	3–28–53	Tan	Portola H.	SINCERELY	
32.	4–25–53	Tan	San Francisco H.	TRUSTING	
33.	5–9–53	Tan	Tanforan H.	TRUSTING	
34.	5–16–53	Hol	Golden State Breeders' H.	ALI'S GEM	
35.	5–23–53	Hol	Hollywood Premiere H.	PET BULLY	
36.	6–9–53	Hol	June Juvenile S.	HEEL FLAME	
37.	6–10–53	Hol	Lakes and Flowers H.	PET BULLY	
38.	6–13–53	Hol	Cinema H.	ALI'S GEM	
39.	6–16–53	Hol	Playa del Rey S.	PERFECTION	
40.	6–17–53	Hol	Cinderella S.	LOVE FACTOR	
41.	7–10–53	Hol	C. S. Howard S.	CORRELATION	
42.	8–15–53	DM	Junior Miss S.	LADY COVER UP	
43.	8–15–53	DM	San Diego H.	GOOSE KHAL	
44.	8–29–53	DM	Del Mar Debutante S.	LADY COVER UP	
45.	9–7–53	DM	Del Mar H.	GOOSE KHAL	
46.	9–10–53	DM	Adios H.	BERSEEM	
47.	9–19–53	GGF	Berkeley H.	BERSEEM	
48.	9–23–53	GGF	Alameda S.	LADY COVER UP	
49.	9–26–53	GGF	Albany H.	GOOSE KHAL	
50.	10–7–53	GGF	Emeryville Primer S.	SUGAR CUBE	

* Key to tracks follows table.
** $100,000 or more added race; totals of these in parentheses at right.

Stakes Races Won by Shoemaker (Continued)

	Date	Track*	Stakes Race	Horse	
51.	10–10 53	GGF	Golden Gate Mile H.	GOOSE KHAL	
52.	11–3–53	BM	Wishing Well H.	VICKI BLUE	
53.	11–7–53	BM	Robert O'Brien H.	DETERMINE	
54.	11–26–53	BM	San Jose H.	IMBROS	
55.	12–30–53	SA	California Breeders' Trial S.	LUCKY MARTIN	
56.	1–6–54	SA	Las Flores H.	VICKI BLUE	
57.	1–23–54	SA	Santa Margarita H.	CERISE REINE	
58.	2–27–54	SA	Santa Anita H.**	REJECTED	(2)
59.	3–20–54	Gulf	Florida Derby**	CORRELATION	(3)
60.	4–19–54	Jam	Jamaica H.	MAGIC LAMP	
61.	4–24–54	Jam	Wood Memorial S.**	CORRELATION	(4)
62.	5–14–54	Hol	Hollywood Premiere H.	STRANGLEHOLD	
63.	5–27–54	Hol	Playa del Rey S.	MILLA'S ABBEY	
64.	6–22–54	Hol	Haggin S.	MR. SULLIVAN	
65.	7–5–54	Hol	American H.	REJECTED	
66.	8–28–54	DM	Del Mar Derby	MUSSELSHELL	
67.	9–4–54	DM	Del Mar Debutante S.	FAIR MOLLY	
68.	9–6–54	DM	Del Mar H.	STRANGLEHOLD	
69.	9–9–54	Sac	Governor's H.	BERSEEM	
70.	9–11–54	DM	Del Mar Futurity	BLUE RULER	
71.	10–9–54	Tan	San Francisco H.	STRANGLEHOLD	
72.	12–31–54	SA	California Breeders' Trial S.	MR. SULLIVAN	
73.	1–1–55	SA	San Pasqual H.	REJECTED	
74.	1–15–55	SA	San Fernando S.	POONA II†	
75.	1–19–55	SA	San Vicente S.	SWAPS	
76.	2–19–55	SA	Los Cerritos H.	FIRST BABY	
77.	2–26–55	SA	Santa Anita H.**	POONA II†	(5)
78.	3–19–55	GGF	Albany H.	GIGANTIC	
79.	4–2–55	GGF	Golden Gate Oaks H.	BELL O'SHANDON	
80.	5–7–55	ChD	Kentucky Derby**	SWAPS	(6)
81.	5–14–55	GGF	Oakland H.	BEAU BUSHER	
82.	5–17–55	Hol	Cabrillo S. (Div. 2)	LIKE MAGIC	
83.	5–21–55	Hol	Debonair S.	BEQUEATH	
84.	5–30–55	Hol	Will Rogers S.	SWAPS	
85.	7–9–55	Hol	Westerner S.	SWAPS	
86.	7–19–55	Hol	El Dorado H.	NEW TREND	
87.	8–1–55	Wash	Clang H.	DUKE'S LEA	
88.	8–3–55	Wash	Mademoiselle S.	GUARD RAIL	
89.	8–20–55	Wash	American Derby**	SWAPS	(7)
90.	8–27–55	Wash	Meadowland H.	DUKE'S LEA	
91.	9–5–55	Wash	Washington Park H.**	JET ACTION	(8)
92.	10–29–55	BM	William P. Kyne H.	MISTER GUS	
93.	12–31–55	SA	California Breeders' Trial S.	TERRANG	
94.	2–4–56	SA	San Vicente H.	TERRANG	
95.	2–14–56	SA	San Luis Rey H.	BLUE VOLT	
96.	2–22–56	SA	Washington's Birthday H.	BLUE VOLT	
97.	3–3–56	SA	Santa Anita Derby**	TERRANG	(9)
98.	3–21–56	Gulf	Suwannee River H.	TREMOR	
99.	5–12–56	Hol	Debonair S.	JOHNIE MIKE	
100.	5–30–56	Hol	Will Rogers S.	TERRANG	

 * Key to tracks follows table.
 ** $100,000 or more added race; totals of these in parentheses at right.
 † Foreign-bred horse.

Stakes Races Won by Shoemaker (Continued)

	Date	Track*	Stakes Race	Horse	
101.	6–9–56	Hol	Argonaut H.	SWAPS	
102.	6–21–56	Hol	Hollywood Oaks	CANDY DISH	
103.	6–23–56	Hol	Inglewood H.	SWAPS	
104.	7–4–56	Hol	American H.**	SWAPS	(10)
105.	7–10–56	Hol	C. S. Howard S.	MR. SAM S.	
106.	7–14–56	Hol	Hollywood Gold Cup**	SWAPS	(11)
107.	7–25–56	Hol	Sunset H.**	SWAPS	(12)
108.	8–1–56	Wash	Mademoiselle S.	ROMANITE	
109.	8–4–56	Wash	Sheridan H.	BEN A. JONES	
110.	8–11–56	Wash	Meadowland H.	MAHAN†	
111.	8–22–56	Wash	Prairie State S.	CALIFORNIA KID	
112.	9–3–56	Wash	Washington Park H.**	SWAPS	(13)
113.	10–6–56	AtlC	Absecon Island S.	CLEM	
114.	10–12–56	Bel	Ladies H.	FLOWER BOWL	
115.	10–17–56	GSt	New Jersey Breeders' S.	AMBEHAVING	
116.	11–24–56	BM	Mapes Hotel H.	CARDIFF	
117.	12–15–56	BM	Bay Meadows H.	HOLANDES II†	
118.	1–9–57	SA	La Centinela S.	ROYAL RASHER	
119.	1–12–57	SA	El Encino H.	BLUE VOLT	
120.	1–12–57	SA	San Fernando S.	HOLANDES II†	
121.	1–30–57	SA	Santa Maria H.	KINGS MISTAKE	
122.	2–12–57	SA	San Luis Rey H.	POSADAS†	
123.	3–23–57	BM	Salinas H.	ROYAL CLIPPER	
124.	5–24–57	Hol	Junior League S.	GLORIOUS NYMPH	
125.	5–25–57	Hol	Californian S. **	SOCIAL CLIMBER	(14)
126.	6–4–57	Hol	Honeymoon S. (Div. 1)	GREAT PRIDE	
127.	6–6–57	Hol	Cinderella S.	GLORIOUS NYMPH	
128.	6–11–57	Hol	Haggin S.	MUSIC MAN FOX	
129.	6–15–57	Bel	Belmont S.**	GALLANT MAN†	(15)
130.	7–1–57	Bel	Peter Pan H.	GALLANT MAN†	
131.	7–6–57	Hol	Cinema H.	ROUND TABLE	
132.	7–13–57	Hol	Hollywood Gold Cup**	ROUND TABLE	(16)
133.	7–20–57	Hol	Westerner S.**	ROUND TABLE	(17)
134.	7–24–57	Arl	Arlington Matron H.	PUCKER UP	
135.	8–17–57	Sara	Travers S.	GALLANT MAN†	
136.	8–26–57	Wash	Clang H.	FLIGHT HISTORY	
137.	8–31–57	Wash	American Derby**	ROUND TABLE	(18)
138.	9–2–57	Wash	Washington Park H.**	PUCKER UP	(19)
139.	9–14–57	AtlC	United Nations H.**	ROUND TABLE	(20)
140.	9–18–57	Bel	Nassau County H.	GALLANT MAN†	
141.	9–21–57	Bel	Beldame H.	PUCKER UP	
142.	10–12–57	Bel	Jockey Club Gold Cup	GALLANT MAN†	
143.	10–12–57	Bel	Champagne S.	JEWEL'S REWARD	
144.	11–23–57	Pim	Pimlico Futurity	JEWEL'S REWARD	
145.	12–26–57	SA	Palos Verdes H.	NASHVILLE	
146.	12–28–57	SA	Malibu Sequet S.	ROUND TABLE	
147.	1–1–58	SA	Las Flores H.	BALLET KHAL	
148.	1–11–58	SA	San Fernando S.	ROUND TABLE	
149.	2–1–58	SA	San Marcos H.	EKABA	
150.	2–15–58	SA	San Antonio H.	ROUND TABLE	
151.	3–1–58	SA	Santa Anita H.**	ROUND TABLE	(21)

---

* Key to tracks follows table.
** $100,000 or more added race; totals of these in parentheses at right.
† Foreign-bred horse.

Stakes Races Won by Shoemaker (Continued)

	Date	Track*	Stakes Race	Horse	
152.	3–8 58	SA	Santa Anita Derby **	SILKY SULLIVAN	(22)
153.	3–28–58	Gulf	Gulfstream Park H.**	ROUND TABLE	(23)
154.	4–12–58	GGF	Golden Poppy H.	MYRTLE	
155.	5–10–58	Hol	Debonair S.	OLD PUEBLO	
156.	5–11–58	AC	Caliente H.	ROUND TABLE	
157.	5–28–58	Hol	Haggin S.	TOMY LEE†	
158.	6–7–58	Hol	Argonaut H.	ROUND TABLE	
159.	6–14–58	Bel	Metropolitan H.	GALLANT MAN†	
160.	6–24–58	Hol	C. S. Howard S.	TOMY LEE†	
161.	6–28–58	Wash	Arch Ward Memorial H.	ROUND TABLE	
162.	7–5–58	Hol	Cinema H.	THE SHOE	
163.	7–11–58	Hol	Coronado H.	CARONAT	
164.	7–12–58	Hol	Hollywood Gold Cup**	GALLANT MAN†	(24)
165.	7–17–58	Hol	Starlet S.	TOMY LEE†	
166.	7–28–58	Hol	Sunset H.**	GALLANT MAN†	(25)
167.	8–2–58	Arl	Arlington Futurity	RESTLESS WIND	
168.	8–6–58	Arl	Cleopatra H. (Div. 1)	MUNCH	
169.	8–6–58	Arl	Cleopatra H. (Div. 2)	MILLY K.	
170.	8–18–58	Arl	Prairie State S.	RESTLESS WIND	
171.	8–23–58	Arl	Arlington H.	ROUND TABLE	
172.	8–30–58	Arl	Washington Park Futurity	RESTLESS WIND	
173.	9–6–58	DM	Del Mar Futurity	TOMY LEE†	
174.	9–13–58	AtlC	United Nations H.**	CLEM	(26)
175.	9–17–58	Bel	Nassau County H.	EDDIE SCHMIDT	
176.	9–20–58	Bel	Belmont Futurity	INTENTIONALLY	
177.	9–27–58	Bel	Woodward S.**	CLEM	(27)
178.	10–1–58	Bel	Lawrence Realization	MARTINS RULLAH	
179.	10–11–58	Haw	Hawthorne Gold Cup**	ROUND TABLE	(28)
180.	10–18–58	Bel	Vosburgh H.	TICK TOCK	
181.	10–20–58	Bel	New York H.	ANXIOUS MOMENT	
182.	11–22–58	Pim	Pimlico Futurity	INTENTIONALLY	
183.	12–31–58	SA	Los Feliz S.	ROYAL ORBIT	
184.	1–24–59	SA	San Marcos H.	ROUND TABLE	
185.	2–4–59	SA	San Pasqual H.	TEMPEST II†	
186.	2–25–59	SA	C. J. Fitzgerald H.	SWIRLING ABBEY	
187.	4–4–59	Jam	Paumonok H.	ISENDU	
188.	4–23–59	Keen	Blue Grass S.	TOMY LEE†	
189.	4–25–59	ChD	Oaks Prep	RUWENZORI	
190.	5–2–59	ChD	Kentucky Derby**	TOMY LEE†	(29)
191.	5–26–59	Hol	Nursery S.	NASCANIA	
192.	5–30–59	Bel	Metropolitan H.**	SWORD DANCER	(30)
193.	6–8–59	Bel	Top Flight H.	BIG EFFORT	
194.	6–13–59	Bel	Belmont S.**	SWORD DANCER	(31)
195.	6–27–59	Hol	Hollywood Derby **	BAGDAD	(32)
196.	6–30–59	Hol	Hollywood Lassie S.	ECHOIC	
197.	7–3–59	Hol	Milady H.	HONEYS GEM	
198.	7–4–59	Wash	Stars and Stripes H.	ROUND TABLE	
199.	7–16–59	Hol	Vanity H. (Div. 1)	TENDER SIZE	
200.	7–16–59	Hol	Vanity H. (Div. 2)	ZEVS JOY	
201.	7–25–59	Mon	Monmouth H.**	SWORD DANCER	(33)
202.	8–22–59	Arl	Arlington H.**	ROUND TABLE	(34)
203.	8–27–59	Arl	Abraham Lincoln S.	OFFICIAL SEAL	

* Key to tracks follows table.
** $100,000 or more added race; totals of these in parentheses at right.
† Foreign-bred horse.

Stakes Races Won by Shoemaker (Continued)

	Date	Track*	Stakes Race	Horse	
204.	8–29–59	Sara	Hopeful S.	TOMPION	
205.	9–7–59	Arl	Washington Park H.**	ROUND TABLE	(35)
206.	9–9–59	Bel	Gazelle H. (Div. 1)	SUNSET GLOW	
207.	9–19–59	AtlC	United Nations H.**	ROUND TABLE	(36)
208.	9–28–59	Aqu	Long Island H. (Div. 2)	ONE-EYED KING	
209.	10–10–59	Aqu	Manhattan H.	ROUND TABLE	
210.	10–28–59	Aqu	Interborough H.	NUSHIE	
211.	12–26–59	SA	Palos Verdes H.	CLANDESTINE	
212.	12–26–59	SA	California Breeders' Trial S.	T.V. LARK	
213.	12–31–59	SA	Los Feliz S.	NEW POLICY	
214.	1–14–60	SA	San Miguel S.	NEW POLICY	
215.	1–19–60	SA	Santa Ynez S.	SOLID THOUGHT	
216.	2–12–60	SA	California Breeders' Champion S.	NEW POLICY	
217.	2–13–60	SA	San Antonio H.	BAGDAD	
218.	3–5–60	SA	Santa Anita Derby**	TOMPION	(37)
219.	4–9–60	Lau	Laurel Maturity	FIRST LANDING	
220.	4–23–60	Aqu	Wood Memorial S.	FRANCIS S.	
221.	4–28–60	Keen	Blue Grass S.	TOMPION	
222.	5–26–60	Hol	Cabrillo S.	DANCE LESSON	
223.	6–16–60	Hol	Milady H.	SILVER SPOON	
224.	6–18–60	Hol	Inglewood H.	BAGDAD	
225.	6–25–60	Hol	Cinema H.	NEW POLICY	
226.	7–12–60	Hol	C. S. Howard S.	OLDEN TIMES	
227.	7–21–60	Hol	Lakes and Flowers H.	ALIWAR	
228.	8–6–60	Arl	Laurance Armour Memorial H.	DOTTED SWISS	
229.	10–22–60	GSt	Gardenia S.	BOWL OF FLOWERS	
230.	11–2–60	Aqu	Knickerbocker H.	QUIZ STAR	
231.	11–5–60	Aqu	Roamer H.	DIVINE COMEDY	
232.	12–26–60	SA	Palos Verdes H.	OLE FOLS†	
233.	1–12–61	SA	Santa Monica H. (Div. 1)	TABOO	
234.	1–12–61	SA	Santa Monica H. (Div. 2)	SWISS ROLL	
235.	1–14–61	SA	San Fernando S.	PROVE IT	
236.	1–19–61	SA	Santa Ynez S.	HET'S PET	
237.	1–28–61	SA	Santa Anita Maturity**	PROVE IT	(38)
238.	2–8–61	SA	California Breeders' Champion S.	OLDEN TIMES	
239.	2–13–61	SA	San Luis Rey H.	DON'T ALIBI	
240.	2–25–61	SA	Santa Anita H.**	PROVE IT	(39)
241.	3–8–61	SA	San Bernardino H.	NEW POLICY	
242.	3–11–61	SA	San Juan Capistrano H.**	DON'T ALIBI	(40)
243.	5–13–61	Hol	Debonair S.	OLDEN TIMES	
244.	5–29–61	Hol	Honeymoon S.	BUSHEL-N-PECK	
245.	7–15–61	Dela	Delaware Oaks	PRIMONETTA	
246.	8–5–61	Sara	Alabama S.	PRIMONETTA	
247.	8–19–61	Sara	Saratoga H.	DIVINE COMEDY	
248.	9–9–61	Bel	Matron S.	CICADA	
249.	9–25–61	Bel	Astarita S.	CICADA	
250.	9–27–61	Bel	Discovery H.	AMBIOPOISE	
251.	10–7–61	Aqu	Frizette S.	CICADA	
252.	10–21–61	GSt	Gardenia S.	CICADA	
253.	11–4–61	GSt	Garden State S.**	CRIMSON SATAN	(41)
254.	11–11–61	Aqu	Roamer H.	SHERLUCK	

* Key to tracks follows table.
** $100,000 or more added race; totals of these in parentheses at right.
† Foreign-bred horse.

Stakes Races Won by Shoemaker (Continued)

	Date	Track*	Stakes Race	Horse	
255.	11–18–61	Pim	Pimlico Futurity	CRIMSON SATAN	
256.	12–30–61	SA	Malibu S.	OLDEN TIMES	
257.	12–30–61	SA	California Breeders' Champion S.	NAJIN	
258.	1–25–62	SA	Santa Ynez S.	DON'T LINGER	
259.	1–30–62	SA	Santa Catalina H.	NEW POLICY	
260.	2–22–62	SA	Washington's Birthday H.	THE AXE II	
261.	3–10–62	SA	San Juan Capistrano H.**	OLDEN TIMES	(42)
262.	3–21–62	Gulf	Fountain of Youth S.	SHARP COUNT	
263.	4–7–62	Aqu	Gotham S.	JAIPUR	
264.	4–28–62	ChD	Oaks Prep	CICADA	
265.	5–3–62	ChD	Churchill Downs H.	EDITORIALIST	
266.	5–4–62	ChD	Kentucky Oaks	CICADA	
267.	5–5–62	ChD	Debutante S.	SPEEDWELL	
268.	5–12–62	Aqu	Withers S.	JAIPUR	
269.	5–19–62	Aqu	Acorn S.	CICADA	
270.	6–2–62	Bel	Mother Goose S.	CICADA	
271.	6–7–62	Hol	Golden State Breeders' H.	OLDEN TIMES	
272.	6–9–62	Bel	Belmont S.**	JAIPUR	(43)
273.	6–14–62	Hol	Cinderella S.	HONEY BUNNY	
274.	6–16–62	Bel	Nassau County S.	BEAU PRINCE	
275.	7–3–62	Hol	Hollywood Lassie S.	HONEY BUNNY	
276.	7–12–62	Hol	C. S. Howard S.	SPACE SKATES	
277.	7–19–62	Hol	Lakes and Flowers H.	WALLET LIFTER	
278.	7–23–62	Hol	Sunset H.	PROVE IT	
279.	8–1–62	Mon	Choice S.	JAIPUR	
280.	8–18–62	Sara	Travers S.	JAIPUR	
281.	8–20–62	Arl	Reigh Count S.	BLUE TASSLE	
282.	8–22–62	Arl	Futurity Trial (Div. 1)	CANDY SPOTS	
283.	8–22–62	Arl	Futurity Trial (Div. 2)	SPACE SKATES	
284.	8–25–62	Arl	Arlington Matron H.	KOOTENAI	
285.	9–3–62	Arl	Washington Park H.**	PROVE IT	(44)
286.	9–8–62	Arl	Arlington-Washington Futurity**	CANDY SPOTS	(45)
287.	9–15–62	Aqu	Futurity S.	NEVER BEND	
288.	9–22–62	Aqu	Beldame S.	CICADA	
289.	10–8–62	Bel	Long Island H. (Div. 1)	THE AXE II	
290.	10–17–62	Bel	Knickerbocker H.	THE AXE II	
291.	10–18–62	Keen	Spinster S.	PRIMONETTA	
292.	11–6–62	Aqu	Interborough H.	WINDY MISS	
293.	11–10–62	GSt	Garden State S.**	CREWMAN	(46)
294.	12–29–62	SA	California Breeders' Champion S.	KINGOMINE	
295.	12–31–62	SA	Las Flores H.	OIL ROYALTY	
296.	1–8–63	SA	Los Feliz S.	TURF CHARGER	
297.	1–10–63	SA	Santa Monica H.	TABLE MATE	
298.	1–29–63	SA	San Pasqual H.	OLDEN TIMES	
299.	3–2–63	SA	Santa Anita Derby**	CANDY SPOTS	(47)
300.	3–23–63	Gulf	Donn H.	TUTANKHAMEN	
301.	3–30–63	Gulf	Florida Derby**	CANDY SPOTS	(48)
302.	4–10–63	Aqu	Prioress S.	SPEEDWELL	
303.	4–17–63	Aqu	Distaff H.	CICADA	
304.	4–30–63	ChD	Derby Trial S.	BONJOUR	
305.	5–18–63	Pim	Preakness S.**	CANDY SPOTS	(49)
306.	5–21–63	Hol	Cabrillo S.	WIL RAD	

* Key to tracks follows table.
** $100,000 or more added race; totals of these in parentheses at right.

Stakes Races Won by Shoemaker (Continued)

	Date	Track*	Stakes Race	Horse	
307.	5–30–63	GSt	Jersey Derby**	CANDY SPOTS	(50)
308.	6–6–63	Hol	Coronado H.	WINDY SEA	
309.	6–11–63	Hol	Wilshire H.	EDIE BELLE	
310.	6–27–63	Hol	Haggin S. (Div. 1)	THE SCOUNDREL	
311.	6–29–63	Hol	Vanity H.	TABLE MATE	
312.	7–4–63	Hol	American H.	DR. KACY	
313.	7–11–63	Hol	C. S. Howard S. (Div. 1)	CLOSE BY	
314.	7–13–63	Arl	American Derby**	CANDY SPOTS	(51)
315.	7–16–63	Hol	Hollywood Oaks	DELHI MAID	
316.	7–22–63	Hol	Lakes and Flowers H.	WINDY SEA	
317.	8–3–63	Arl	Arlington Classic**	CANDY SPOTS	(52)
318.	8–14–63	Arl	Princess Pat S.	SARI'S SONG	
319.	8–20–63	Arl	Marion H.	ABBY'S CROWN	
320.	8–31–63	Arl	Arlington-Washington Lassie S.**	SARI'S SONG	(53)
321.	9–4–63	Arl	Warren Wright H.	QUEST LINK	
322.	9–23–63	Aqu	Discovery H.	QUEST LINK	
323.	10–7–63	Aqu	Long Island H.	DAVID K.	
324.	10–24–63	Aqu	Knickerbocker H. (Div. 1)	PARKA	
325.	11–16–63	GGF	Richmond H.	HARRY H.	
326.	12–7–63	GGF	San Francisco Mile H.	NATIVE DIVER	
327.	12–21–63	GGF	Golden Gate H.	NATIVE DIVER	
328.	1–15–64	SA	San Fernando S. (Div. 2)	GUN BOW	
329.	1–16–64	SA	San Miguel S.	REAL GOOD DEAL	
330.	1–21–64	SA	San Pasqual H.	OLDEN TIMES	
331.	1–25–64	SA	Charles H. Strub S.**	GUN BOW	(54)
332.	1–28–64	SA	San Vicente H.	WIL RAD	
333.	2–8–64	SA	San Antonio H.	GUN BOW	
334.	2–20–64	SA	Santa Susana H.	BLUE NORTHER	
335.	3–3–64	Hia	Flamingo S.**	NORTHERN DANCER	(55)
336.	3–20–64	Aqu	Swift S.	BLACK MOUNTAIN	
337.	3–21–64	Gulf	Gulfstream Park H.**	GUN BOW	(56)
338.	4–4–64	Gulf	Florida Derby**	NORTHERN DANCER	(57)
339.	4–11–64	Keen	Ashland S.	BLUE NORTHER	
340.	4–28–64	ChD	Derby Trial S.	HILL RISE	
341.	4–30–64	ChD	Churchill Downs H.	OLDEN TIMES	
342.	5–1–64	ChD	Kentucky Oaks	BLUE NORTHER	
343.	5–2–64	ChD	Debutante S.	MISSISSIPPI MAMA	
344.	5–19–64	Hol	Goose Girl S.	DUCHESS KHALED	
345.	6–2–64	Hol	Nursery S. (Div. 1)	I SURRENDER	
346.	6–11–64	Hol	Westchester S. (Div. 2)	FLEET SON	
347.	6–20–64	Arl	Illinois H.**	OLDEN TIMES	(58)
348.	6–27–64	Hol	Cinema H.	CLOSE BY	
349.	6–30–64	Hol	Haggin S. (Div. 1)	TER-CHI-BERZO	
350.	6–30–64	Hol	Haggin S. (Div. 2)	FLEET SON	
351.	7–3–64	Hol	Vanity H.	STAR MAGGIE	
352.	7–14–64	Hol	Lakes and Flowers H.	TURLOC	
353.	7–27–64	Hol	Sunset H.	COLORADO KING†	
354.	7–29–64	Arl	Beverly H.	STAR MAGGIE	
355.	9–12–64	Arl	Arlington-Washington Futurity**	SADAIR	(59)
356.	9–23–64	Aqu	Stymie H.	THE IBEX	
357.	10–10–64	Aqu	Frizette S.	QUEEN EMPRESS	
358.	10–21–64	Aqu	Interborough H.	AFFECTIONATELY	

* Key to tracks follows table.
** $100,000 or more added race; totals of these in parentheses at right.
† Foreign-bred horse.

Stakes Races Won by Shoemaker (Continued)

	Date	Track*	Stakes Race	Horse	
359.	11–2–64	Aqu	Sport Page H.	AFFECTIONATELY	
360.	11–7–64	GSt	Gardenia S.	QUEEN EMPRESS	
361.	12–31–64	SA	Las Flores H.	AFFECTIONATELY††	
362.	1–26–65	SA	San Pasqual H.	CANDY SPOTS	
363.	2–2–65	SA	San Vicente H.	LUCKY DEBONAIR	
364.	2–4–65	SA	Arcadia H.	CEDAR KEY	
365.	3–6–65	SA	Santa Anita Derby**	LUCKY DEBONAIR	(60)
366.	4–20–65	Keen	Bewitch S. (Div. 2)	OLE LIZ	
367.	4–22–65	Keen	Blue Grass S.	LUCKY DEBONAIR	
368.	5–1–65	ChD	Debutante S.	OLE LIZ	
369.	5–1–65	ChD	Kentucky Derby**	LUCKY DEBONAIR	(61)
370.	6–12–65	Hol	Argonaut S.	CARPENTERS RULE	
371.	7–13–65	Hol	C. S. Howard S. (Div. 2)	PORT WINE	
372.	7–17–65	Arl	Citation H.	TOM ROLFE	
373.	7–20–65	Hol	El Dorado H.	BLUE SURGE	
374.	7–24–65	Hol	Hollywood Juvenile Championship**	PORT WINE	(62)
375.	7–31–65	Arl	Arlington H.	CHIEFTAIN	
376.	8–4–65	Arl	Pucker Up H.	MINE LOVELY	
377.	8–7–65	Arl	Chicagoan S.**	TOM ROLFE	(63)
378.	8–18–65	Arl	Lassie Trial S.	OLE LIZ	
379.	8–28–65	Arl	Arlington Classic**	TOM ROLFE	(64)
380.	9–2–65	Arl	Prairie State S.	REBEL MAN	
381.	9–13–65	Arl	American Derby**	TOM ROLFE	(65)
382.	1–5–66	SA	Los Feliz S. (Div. 2)	SABER MOUNTAIN	
383.	1–13–66	SA	San Miguel S.	PORT WINE	
384.	1–27–66	SA	San Vicente S.	SABER MOUNTAIN	
385.	1–29–66	SA	Charles H. Strub S.**	BOLD BIDDER	(66)
386.	2–5–66	SA	Santa Margarita H.	STRAIGHT DEAL	
387.	2–19–66	SA	San Luis Rey H. (Div. 2)	CEDAR KEY	
388.	2–22–66	SA	San Felipe H.	SABER MOUNTAIN	
389.	2–23–66	Hia	Everglades S.	BUCKPASSER	
390.	2–24–66	SA	Santa Barbara H.	STRAIGHT DEAL	
391.	2–26–66	SA	Santa Anita H.**	LUCKY DEBONAIR	(67)
392.	3–3–66	Hia	Flamingo S.**	BUCKPASSER	(68)
393.	3–14–66	SA	San Marino H. (Div. 2)	PELEGRIN	
394.	4–8–66	Aqu	Prioress S.	MY BOSS LADY	
395.	4–28–66	Keen	Blue Grass S.	ABE'S HOPE	
396.	5–7–66	ChD	Debutante S.	FURL SAIL	
397.	5–12–66	Hol	Goose Girl S. (Div. 1)	ENGLISH TOFFEE	
398.	5–17–66	Hol	Coronado H.	TOULORE	
399.	5–19–66	Hol	Cabrillo S.	RESTLESS SONG	
400.	5–28–66	Aqu	Acorn S.	MARKING TIME	
401.	6–1–66	Hol	Westchester S.	TUMBLE WIND	
402.	6–7–66	Hol	Wilshire H.	POONA QUEEN	
403.	6–21–66	Hol	C. S. Howard S.	TITLE GAME	
404.	6–25–66	Hol	Cinema H.	DRIN	
405.	6–30–66	Hol	Haggin S.	TUMBLE WIND	
406.	7–4–66	Mon	Monmouth Oaks	NATASHKA	
407.	7–14–66	Hol	Portola S.	TITLE GAME	
408.	8–3–66	Mon	Salvator Mile H.	TOM ROLFE	
409.	8–6–66	Mon	Sapling S.	GREAT POWER	

* Key to tracks follows table.
** $100,000 or more added race; totals of these in parentheses at right.
†† Dead heat.

Stakes Races Won by Shoemaker (Continued)

	Date	Track*	Stakes Race	Horse	
410.	8–13–66	Sara	Alabama S.	NATASHKA	
411.	9–5–66	Aqu	Aqueduct H.**	TOM ROLFE	(69)
412.	9–10–66	Arl	Arlington-Washington Futurity**	DIPLOMAT WAY	(70)
413.	10–5–66	Aqu	Cowdin S.	DR. FAGER	
414.	10–10–66	Aqu	Discovery H.	DECK HAND	
415.	10–17–66	Aqu	Interborough H.	NATIVE STREET	
416.	11–30–66	Aqu	Remsen S.	DAMASCUS	
417.	12–26–66	SA	Palos Verdes H.	PRETENSE	
418.	12–28–66	SA	Las Flores H.	NATASHKA	
419.	1–21–67	SA	Santa Maria H.	NATASHKA	
420.	1–21–67	SA	San Marcos H.	REHABILITATE	
421.	1–26–67	SA	San Pasqual H.	PRETENSE	
422.	2–9–67	SA	San Vicente S.	TUMBLE WIND	
423.	2–11–67	SA	San Antonio H.	PRETENSE	
424.	2–13–67	SA	Santa Susana S.	FISH HOUSE	
425.	2–18–67	SA	San Luis Rey H. (Div. 1)	NIARKOS†	
426.	2–18–67	SA	San Luis Rey H. (Div. 2)	FLEET HOST	
427.	2–23–67	SA	Santa Barbara H. (Div. 1)	APRIL DAWN	
428.	2–25–67	SA	Santa Anita H.**	PRETENSE	(71)
429.	2–28–67	SA	Sierra Madre H.	SABER MOUNTAIN	
430.	3–25–67	Aqu	Bay Shore S.	DAMASCUS	
431.	4–22–67	Aqu	Wood Memorial S.**	DAMASCUS	(72)
432.	4–29–67	ChD	La Troienne S.	FURL SAIL	
433.	5–10–67	Hol	Premiere H.	FLEET DISCOVERY	
434.	5–16–67	Hol	Coronado S.	FORLI†	
435.	5–20–67	Pim	Preakness S.**	DAMASCUS	(73)
436.	5–27–67	Hol	Hollypark Ladies H. (Div. 1)	APRIL DAWN	
437.	5–29–67	Aqu	Juvenile S.	KASKASKIA	
438.	6–1–67	Hol	Nursery S.	MORGAISE	
439.	6–3–67	Aqu	Belmont S.**	DAMASCUS	(74)
440.	6–10–67	Hol	Argonaut S. (Div. 2)	TUMBLE WIND	
441.	6–29–67	Hol	Cortez H.	HILL CLOWN	
442.	7–3–67	Hol	Princess S.	GAMELY	
443.	7–6–67	Hol	Hollywood Lassie S.	MORGAISE	
444.	7–15–67	Aqu	Dwyer S.	DAMASCUS	
445.	7–24–67	Hol	Sunset H.**	HILL CLOWN	(75)
446.	7–31–67	Arl	Majorette S.	SNAPPY QUILLO	
447.	8–5–67	Arl	American Derby**	DAMASCUS	(76)
448.	8–12–67	Sara	Alabama S.	GAMELY	
449.	8–19–67	Sara	Travers S.	DAMASCUS	
450.	9–4–67	Aqu	Aqueduct S.**	DAMASCUS	(77)
451.	9–9–67	Arl	Arlington-Washington Futurity (Div. 2)	VITRIOLIC	
452.	9–11–67	Arl	Chicagoan S.	MINNESOTA MAC	
453.	9–23–67	Aqu	Futurity S.	CAPTAIN'S GIG	
454.	9–30–67	Aqu	Woodward S.**	DAMASCUS	(78)
455.	10–9–67	Aqu	Discovery H.	BOLD HOUR	
456.	10–21–67	Aqu	Jockey Club Gold Cup**	DAMASCUS	(79)
457.	1–6–68	SA	Malibu S.	DAMASCUS	
458.	1–16–68	SA	Camino Real H. (Div. 1)	PASS THE BRANDY	
459.	1–16–68	SA	Camino Real H. (Div. 2)	MODEL FOOL	
460.	1–20–68	SA	San Fernando S.	DAMASCUS	

* Key to tracks follows table.
** $100,000 or more added race; totals of these in parentheses at right.
† Foreign-bred horse.

Stakes Races Won by Shoemaker (Continued)

	Date	Track*	Stakes Race	Horse	
461.	2–18–69	SA	Santa Catalina S.	INVERNESS DRIVE	
462.	2–25–69	SA	Santa Ynez S.	POONA DOWNS	
463.	3–13–69	SA	Santa Susana S.	DUMPTY'S LADY	
464.	3–27–69	SA	Baldwin S.	TELL	
465.	4–1–69	SA	San Bernardino H.	PINJARA	
466.	4–19–69	Hol	Century H.	PINJARA	
467.	4–21–69	GGF	Native Diver S.	BERRY PATCH	
468.	4–24–69	Keen	Blue Grass S.	ARTS AND LETTERS	
469.	4–26–69	Hol	Will Rogers S.	TELL	
470.	8–13–69	Arl	Lassie Trial S.	CLOVER LANE	
471.	9–1–69	Arl	Arlington-Washington Lassie S.	CLOVER LANE	
472.	9–8–69	Arl	Laurance Armour H.	LOSTALO†	
473.	9–27–69	BM	Leland Stanford H.	TRIPLE TUX	
474.	10–7–69	SA	Autumn Days S.	TELL	
475.	10–8–69	SA	Anoakia S.	SAILORS MATE	
476.	10–11–69	SA	Carleton F. Burke Invitational H.	FIDDLE ISLE	
477.	10–18–69	SA	Volante H.	TELL	
478.	2–3–70	SA	Oneonta H.	EVERYTHING LOVELY	
479.	2–10–70	SA	Santa Catalina S.	COLORADO KING JR.	
480.	3–14–70	SA	San Felipe H. (Div. 2)	TERLAGO	
481.	3–21–70	SA	San Luis Rey H. (Div. 1)	FIDDLE ISLE	
482.	3–28–70	SA	Santa Anita Derby**	TERLAGO	(80)
483.	4–4–70	SA	San Juan Capistrano Invitational H.**	FIDDLE ISLE††	(81)
484.	4–8–70	SA	San Marino H.	T.V. COMMERCIAL	
485.	4–14–70	Hol	Goose Girl S.	BOLD JIL	
486.	4–16–70	Hol	Coronado S.	PINJARA	
487.	5–9–70	Hol	Argonaut S. (Div. 1)	WESTERN WELCOME	
488.	5–9–70	Hol	Argonaut S. (Div. 2)	COLORADO KING JR.	
489.	5–21–70	Hol	Railbird S.	BOLD JIL	
490.	5–30–70	Hol	Lakeside H.	FIDDLE ISLE	
491.	6–20–70	Hol	Hollywood Invitational Turf H.**	FIDDLE ISLE	(82)
492.	6–30–70	Hol	Portola S.	RIVER ISLE	
493.	7–3–70	Hol	Beverly Hills H.	PATTEE CANYON	
494.	7–4–70	Hol	American H.	FIDDLE ISLE	
495.	7–29–70	DM	Oceanside H.	RULLAH FOLS	
496.	8–7–70	DM	Junior Miss S.	CONNIVING PRINCESS	
497.	8–14–70	DM	C.T.B.A. Sales S.	KFAR TOV	
498.	8–19–70	DM	Del Mar Oaks (Div. 1)	BEJA	
499.	8–24–70	DM	De Anza S.	KFAR TOV	
500.	9–2–70	DM	Osunitas S.	QUEEN JANINE	
501.	10–6–70	SA	Autumn Days H.	ACK ACK	
502.	10–10–70	SA	Carleton F. Burke Invitational H.	FIDDLE ISLE	
503.	10–13–70	SA	Sunny Slope S.	JEANENES LARK	
504.	10–15–70	SA	Linda Vista H.	BEJA	
505.	10–21–70	SA	Volante H.	MICKEY McGUIRE	
506.	1–1–71	SA	San Gabriel H.	COUGAR II†	
507.	1–5–71	SA	Los Feliz S.	SINGLE AGENT	
508.	1–14–71	SA	San Miguel S.	TOWER EAST	
509.	1–16–71	SA	San Carlos H.	ACK ACK	
510.	1–23–71	SA	San Marcos H.	COUGAR II†	

---

* Key to tracks follows table.
** $100,000 or more added race; totals of these in parentheses at right.
† Foreign-bred horse.
†† Dead heat.

Stakes Races Won by Shoemaker (Continued)

	Date	Track*	Stakes Race	Horse	
511.	2-6-71	SA	San Pasqual H.	ACK ACK	
512.	2-18-71	SA	Santa Ynez S.	TURKISH TROUSERS	
513.	2-27-71	SA	San Antonio S.	ACK ACK	
514.	3-4-71	SA	Sierra Madre H.	PINJARA	
515.	3-11-71	SA	Santa Susana S.	TURKISH TROUSERS	
516.	3-13-71	SA	Santa Anita H.**	ACK ACK	(83)
517.	4-10-71	SA	San Juan Capistrano Invitational H.**	COUGAR II†	(84)
518.	4-15-71	Hol	Goose Girl S.	ULLA BRITTA	
519.	4-23-71	Hol	Crenshaw S.	PINJARA	
520.	4-27-71	Hol	Senorita S.	TURKISH TROUSERS	
521.	5-13-71	Hol	Cortez H.	ADVANCE GUARD	
522.	5-18-71	Hol	Railbird S.	TURKISH TROUSERS	
523.	5-22-71	Hol	Californian S.**	COUGAR II†	(85)
524.	6-3-71	Hol	Honeymoon S.	TURKISH TROUSERS	
525.	6-8-71	Hol	Marina del Rey S.	RESTLESS RUNNER	
526.	6-12-71	Hol	Inglewood H.	ADVANCE GUARD	
527.	6-15-71	Hol	Haggin S.	ROYAL CHAMPION	
528.	6-17-71	Hol	Hollywood Express H.	ACK ACK	
529.	6-26-71	Hol	Ford Pinto Invitational H.**	COUGAR II†	(86)
530.	6-29-71	Hol	Cinderella S.	MISS LADY BUG	
531.	7-2-71	Hol	Princess S.	TURKISH TROUSERS	
532.	7-5-71	Hol	American H.	ACK ACK	
533.	7-17-71	Hol	Hollywood Gold Cup Invitational H.**	ACK ACK	(87)
534.	7-22-71	Hol	Hollywood Oaks	TURKISH TROUSERS	
535.	7-24-71	Hol	Hollywood Juvenile Championship**	ROYAL OWL	(88)
536.	7-28-71	DM	Palomar H.	STREET DANCER	
537.	7-30-71	DM	Graduation S.	HOUSE OF PORTER	
538.	7-31-71	DM	San Diego H.	ADVANCE GUARD	
539.	8-13-71	DM	C.T.B.A. Sales S.	MacARTHUR PARK	
540.	8-25-71	DM	Del Mar Oaks	TURKISH TROUSERS	
541.	8-27-71	DM	De Anza S.	MacARTHUR PARK	
542.	9-11-71	DM	Del Mar H.	PINJARA	
543.	9-15-71	DM	Del Mar Futurity	MacARTHUR PARK	
544.	10-7-71	SA	Anoakia S.	MISS LADY BUG	
545.	10-13-71	SA	Sunny Slope S.	MacARTHUR PARK	
546.	10-23-71	SA	Norfolk S.	MacARTHUR PARK	
547.	10-25-71	SA	Las Palmas H.	TYPECAST	
548.	10-30-71	SA	Oak Tree Invitational**	COUGAR II†	(89)
549.	11-13-71	BM	Junipero Serra S.	ROYAL OWL	
550.	12-18-71	BM	California Juvenile S.**	ROYAL OWL	(90)
551.	12-31-71	SA	California Breeders' Champion S.	ROYAL OWL	
552.	1-8-72	SA	Malibu S. (Div. 2)	WING OUT	
553.	2-3-72	SA	Arcadia H. (Div. 1)	BUZKASHI	
554.	2-12-72	SA	Charles H. Strub S.**	UNCONSCIOUS	(91)
555.	2-19-72	SA	Santa Maria H.	TURKISH TROUSERS	
556.	2-21-72	SA	San Luis Obispo H. (Div. 1)	PRACTICANTE†	
557.	2-21-72	SA	San Luis Obispo H. (Div. 2)	LORD DERBY	
558.	3-2-72	SA	San Jacinto S.	ROYAL OWL	
559.	3-4-72	SA	Santa Margarita H.**	TURKISH TROUSERS	(92)
560.	4-4-72	SA	Santa Ana H.	STREET DANCER	
561.	4-15-72	Hol	Will Rogers S.	QUACK	
562.	4-22-72	GGF	California Derby**	QUACK	(93)

* Key to tracks follows table.
** $100,000 or more added race; totals of these in parentheses at right.
† Foreign-bred horse.

Stakes Races Won by Shoemaker (Continued)

	Date	Track*	Stakes Race	Horse	
563.	4–29–72	Hol	Century H.**	COUGAR II†	(94)
564.	5–20–72	Hol	Californian S.**	COUGAR II†	(95)
565.	5–23–72	Hol	Nursery S.	KADESH	
566.	5–26–72	Hol	Manchester Claiming S.	LE LEVANHOT†	
567.	7–4–72	Hol	American H.	BUZKASHI	
568.	7–8–72	Hol	Beverly Hills H.	HILL CIRCUS	
569.	7–11–72	Hol	El Dorado H.	SOLAR SALUTE	
570.	7–12–72	Hol	Hollywood Lassie S.	WINDY'S DAUGHTER	
571.	7–20–72	Hol	Hollywood Oaks	PALLISIMA	
572.	8–18–72	DM	Sorrento S.	WINDY'S DAUGHTER	
573.	8–25–72	DM	De Anza S.	LUCKY MIKE	
574.	9–4–72	DM	Del Mar Debutante S.	WINDY'S DAUGHTER	
575.	9–13–72	DM	Del Mar Futurity	GROSHAWK	
576.	10–9–72	SA	Linda Vista H.	PALLISIMA	
577.	10–28–72	SA	Norfolk S.	GROSHAWK	
578.	11–1–72	SA	Oak Tree Invitational**	COUGAR II†	(96)
579.	1–4–73	SA	La Centinela S. (Div. 2)	TALLAHTO	
580.	1–9–73	SA	Los Feliz S.	PLENTY OF STYLE	
581.	1–23–73	SA	El Monte H.	STAR OF KUWAIT	
582.	4–14–73	Hol	Lakeside H.	WING OUT	
583.	5–5–73	Hol	Century H.**	COUGAR II†	(97)
584.	5–9–73	Hol	Westwood S.	ROD	
585.	5–19–73	Hol	Will Rogers H.	GROSHAWK	
586.	5–20–73	Hol	Cortez H.	MANITOULIN	
587.	6–13–73	Hol	Cygnet S.	LADY BY CHOICE	
588.	6–24–73	Hol	Hollywood Gold Cup Invitational H.**	KENNEDY ROAD†	(98)
589.	7–18–73	Hol	Lakes and Flowers H.	BRIARTIC†	
590.	7–22–73	Hol	Beverly Hills H.	LE CLE	
591.	7–23–73	Hol	Sunset H.**	COUGAR II†	(99)
592.	7–25–73	DM	Palomar H. (Div. 2)	BELLE MARIE	
593.	7–28–73	DM	Oceanside H.	EXPRESSION	
594.	7–29–73	DM	San Diego H.	KENNEDY ROAD†	
595.	8–10–73	DM	C.T.B.A. S.	SUCH A RUSH	
596.	8–11–73	DM	Bing Crosby H.	PATAHA PRINCE	
597.	8–12–73	DM	La Jolla Mile H.	GROSHAWK	
598.	8–18–73	DM	Cabrillo H.	KENNEDY ROAD†	
599.	8–24–73	DM	De Anza S.	SUCH A RUSH	
600.	9–8–73	DM	Chula Vista H.	GROTONIAN	
601.	9–12–73	DM	Del Mar Futurity	SUCH A RUSH	
602.	10–11–73	SA	Autumn Days H.	NEW MOON II†	
603.	10–13–73	SA	Linda Vista H.	LA ZANZARA†	
604.	10–18–73	SA	Sunny Slope S.	SUCH A RUSH	
605.	1–13–74	SA	San Gorgonio Claiming S.	MARGUM	
606.	1–30–74	SA	Pasadena S.	SPECIAL TEAM	
607.	2–2–74	SA	San Pasqual H.	TRI JET	
608.	2–27–74	SA	Santa Ysabel S.	MISS MUSKET	
609.	3–9–74	SA	Santa Susana S.	MISS MUSKET	
610.	3–20–74	SA	El Encino H.	WILD WORLD	
611.	3–30–74	Oak	Fantasy S.**	MISS MUSKET	(100)
612.	4–7–74	SA	Santa Ana H.	BELLE MARIE	
613.	4–14–74	Hol	Lakeside H.	MATUN†	

* Key to tracks follows table.
** $100,000 or more added race; totals of these in parentheses at right.
† Foreign-bred horse.

Stakes Races Won by Shoemaker (Continued)

	Date	Track*	Stakes Race	Horse	
614.	4–17–74	Hol	Debonair S.	SHIRLEY'S CHAMPION	
615.	4–20–74	GGF	California Derby**	AGITATE	(101)
616.	6–23–74	Hol	Hollywood Gold Cup Invitational H.**	TREE OF KNOWLEDGE	(102)
617.	6–30–74	Hol	Swaps S.**	AGITATE	(103)
618.	7–6–74	Hol	Hollywood Express H.	SHIRLEY'S CHAMPION	
619.	7–14–74	Hol	Hollywood Invitational Derby**	AGITATE	(104)
620.	7–22–74	Hol	Sunset H.**	GRECO II†	(105)
621.	7–28–74	DM	San Diego H.	MATUN†	
622.	8–17–74	DM	Osunitas S. (Div. 2)	READY WIT	
623.	8–28–74	DM	Balboa S.	DIABOLO	
624.	9–1–74	DM	Ramona H.	TIZNA†	
625.	9–2–74	DM	Del Mar Debutante S.	BUBBLEWIN	
626.	9–4–74	DM	El Cajon S.	WITHIN HAIL	
627.	9–11–74	DM	Del Mar Futurity	DIABOLO	
628.	10–6–74	SA	Volante H.	WITHIN HAIL	
629.	12–11–74	BM	Children's Hospital H.	READY WIT	
630.	1–8–75	SA	La Centinela S.	SARSAR	
631.	1–24–75	SA	San Rafael S.	DONNA B QUICK	
632.	1–26–75	SA	San Fernando S.	STARDUST MEL	
633.	2–8–75	SA	San Marcos H.	TROJAN BRONZE	
634.	2–9–75	SA	Charles H. Strub S.**	STARDUST MEL	(106)
635.	2–12–75	SA	Pasadena S.	SARSAR	
636.	2–16–75	SA	Santa Maria H.	GAY STYLE	
637.	2–20–75	SA	Santa Catalina S.	KINALMEAKY	
638.	3–2–75	SA	San Jacinto S.	DIABOLO	
639.	3–9–75	SA	Santa Anita H.**	STARDUST MEL	(107)
640.	3–15–75	SA	Santa Susana S.	SARSAR	
641.	3–23–75	SA	Santa Barbara H.	GAY STYLE	
642.	3–30–75	SA	San Bernardino H.	ROYAL GLINT	
643.	4–13–75	Hol	Inglewood H. (Div. 2)	GAY STYLE	
644.	4–21–75	Aqu	Prioress S.	SARSAR	
645.	5–18–75	Hol	Will Rogers H.	UNIFORMITY	
646.	5–24–75	Aqu	Withers S.	SARSAR	
647.	6–1–75	Hol	Cinema H.	TERETE	
648.	6–7–75	Bel	Belmont S.**	AVATAR	(108)
649.	6–14–75	Hol	Hollywood Oaks	NICOSIA	
650.	7–6–75	Hol	Vanity H.**	DULCIA†	(109)
651.	7–21–75	Hol	Sunset H. (Div. 1)	BARCLAY JOY†	
652.	9–7–75	DM	Ramona H.	DULCIA†	
653.	10–12–75	SA	Carleton F. Burke H. (Div. 1)	TOP COMMAND	
654.	10–15–75	SA	Sunny Slope S.	THERMAL ENERGY	
655.	10–19–75	SA	Oak Tree Invitational**	TOP COMMAND	(110)
656.	10–25–75	SA	Las Palmas H.	CHARGER'S STAR	
657.	11–1–75	SA	Nat'l Thoroughbred Championship**	DULCIA†	(111)
658.	12–31–75	SA	La Brea S. (Div. 1)	FEATHERFOOT	
659.	1–7–76	SA	La Centinela S.	DREAM OF SPRING	
660.	2–14–76	SA	San Vicente S.	THERMAL ENERGY	
661.	2–15–76	SA	La Canada S.	RAISE YOUR SKIRTS	
662.	3–14–76	SA	San Felipe H.	CRYSTAL WATER	
663.	3–24–76	SA	San Marino H. (Div. 1)	STRONG†	
664.	3–27–76	SA	Santa Barbara H.	STRAVINA†	

* Key to tracks follows table.
** $100,000 or more added race; totals of these in parentheses at right.
† Foreign-bred horse.

Stakes Races Won by Shoemaker‡

	Date	Track*	Stakes Race	Horse	
665.	4-1-76	SA	San Rafael S.	VAGABONDA	
666.	4-6-76	SA	La Habra S.	DANCING FEMME	
667.	4-17-76	Hol	Hollywood Derby**	CRYSTAL WATER	(112)
668.	4-21-76	Hol	Brentwood S. (Div. 1)	SWINGTIME	
669.	5-1-76	Hol	Coronado H.	BYNODERM†	
670.	5-2-76	Hol	Inglewood H. (Div. 2)	KING PELLINORE	
671.	5-19-76	Hol	Hawthorne H. (Div. 1)	SWINGTIME	
672.	5-29-76	Hol	Honeymoon H.	CASCAPEDIA	
673.	5-31-76	Hol	Hollywood Invitational Turf H.**	DAHLIA	(113)
674.	6-6-76	Hol	Bel Air H.	RIOT IN PARIS	
675.	7-4-76	Hol	American H.	KING PELLINORE	
676.	7-14-76	Hol	Cabrillo S.	I'M A ZIPPER††	
677.	8-11-76	DM	Junior Miss S.	LULLABY	
678.	8-30-76	Bel	Fall Highweight H. (Div. 2)	HONORABLE MISS	
679.	9-6-76	DM	Del Mar Invitational H.**	RIOT IN PARIS	(114)
680.	9-18-76	Bel	Woodward H.**	FOREGO	(115)

* Key to tracks follows table.
** $100,000 or more added race; totals of these in parentheses at right.
† Foreign-bred horse.
†† Dead heat.
‡ Through September 18, 1976.

Key to Tracks

AC	Agua Caliente	Dela	Delaware Park	Hol	Hollywood Park	SA	Santa Anita
Aqu	Aqueduct	DM	Del Mar	Jam	Jamaica	Sac	Sacramento
Arl	Arlington Park	GGF	Golden Gate Fields	Keen	Keeneland	Sara	Saratoga
AtlC	Atlantic City	GSt	Garden State Park	Lau	Laurel	Tan	Tanforan
Bel	Belmont	Gulf	Gulfstream Park	Mon	Monmouth Park	Wash	Washington Park
BM	Bay Meadows	Haw	Hawthorne Park	Oak	Oaklawn Park		
ChD	Churchill Downs	Hia	Hialeah Park	Pim	Pimlico		

Index